Attention and Listening in the Early Years

of related interest

Fun with Messy Play
Ideas and Activities for Children with Special Needs
Tracey Beckerleg
ISBN 978 1 84310 641 8

Grief in Young Children
A Handbook for Adults
Atle Dyregrov
Foreword by Professor William Yule
ISBN 978 1 84310 650 0

Let's All Listen
Songs for Group Work in Settings that Include Students with Learning Difficulties and Autism
Pat Lloyd
Foreword by Adam Ockelford
ISBN 978 1 84310 583 1

Small Steps Forward
Using Games and Activities to Help Your Pre-School Child with Special Needs
2nd edition
Sarah Newman
Illustrated by Jeanie Mellersh
ISBN 978 1 84310 693 7

Challenge Me!(TM)
Speech and Communication Cards
Amanda Elliott
Illustrated by David Kemp
ISBN 978 1 84310 946 4

Creative Coping Skills for Children
Emotional Support through Arts and Crafts Activities
Bonnie Thomas
Illustrated by Bonnie Thomas
ISBN 978 1 84310 921 1

Children with Emotional and Behavioural Difficulties and Communication Problems
There is always a reason
Melanie Cross
ISBN 978 1 84310 135 2

Classroom Tales
Using Storytelling to Build Emotional, Social and Academic Skills across the Primary Curriculum
Jennifer M Fox Eades
ISBN 978 1 84310 304 2

Attention and Listening in the Early Years

Sharon Garforth

Jessica Kingsley Publishers
London and Philadelphia

First published in 2009
by Jessica Kingsley Publishers
116 Pentonville Road
London N1 9JB, UK
and
400 Market Street, Suite 400
Philadelphia, PA 19106, USA

www.jkp.com

Printed digitally since 2010

Library of Congress Cataloging in Publication Data
Garforth, Sharon.
Attention and listening in the early years / Sharon Garforth.
p. cm.
ISBN 978-1-84905-024-1 (pb : alk. paper) 1. Attention. 2. Listening. I. Title.
BF321.G27 2009
372.21'6--dc22
2008054377

British Library Cataloguing in Publication Data
A CIP catalogue record for this book is available from the British Library

ISBN 978 1 84905 024 1

Acknowledgements

My thanks go to Sue Smith for allowing me to use her adapted version of the rhyme 'Little ripples'.

I would also like to thank Shropshire Council and the Telford and Wrekin Primary Care Trust for their support during the production, trialling and evaluation of the 'Attention and Listening in the Early Years' programme, known locally as 'Listen with Lucy'.

I would like to thank my publishers, Jessica Kingsley, for the considerable amount of hand holding which was required to help me through the experience of getting my first book published.

And, finally, I would like to thank my family for their support and advice, and for being there when I needed them.

Contents

Songs and activities

Preface

Attention and Listening in the Early Years was developed in response to increasing concern from schools nationally that children were entering their reception classes without adequate attention, listening and language skills for accessing the National Curriculum (*Early Years Language Survey of Head Teachers*, National Literacy Trust 2001). Having worked as a speech and language therapist for 20 years, the author realized that it is possible to encourage and develop children's attention and listening from a very young age, as long as activities are at an appropriate developmental stage. By facilitating children's attention and listening skills, we are able to give them a better chance of achieving their potential in communication, speech and language skills, and therefore in learning skills. Consequently the author developed *Attention and Listening in the Early Years* for children aged between two and four years.

Attention and Listening in the Early Years is a programme designed to be run as an alternative to the traditional 'circle time' group. Group sessions include a theme, rhymes and songs, all of which are excellent attention and listening activities in their own right. However, in an 'Attention and Listening in the Early Years' group, the children are taken beyond the stage at which these commonly used circle time activities are sufficient to stretch their skills, by means of carefully devised adjustments made to the songs as well as listening activities and games. The group taps into some of the traditional elements of circle time, but with a difference. Therefore Early Years practitioners should find the new approach in *Attention and Listening in the Early Years* straightforward and accessible.

Introduction

Why run an 'Attention and Listening in the Early Years' group?

The abilities to attend, to listen and to look are prerequisites for all forms of learning, including learning communication, speech and language. In the noisy, busy, television-and-computer-filled world children are brought up in nowadays, they do not always get sufficient opportunities to learn how to concentrate and attend, how to notice and learn from what they hear (listen), and how to notice and learn from what they see (look).

Early Years practitioners are in the ideal position to promote children's auditory (listening) and visual (looking) attention on a regular basis, and so provide them with a better start for their communication and social development, and their learning skills.

When given the opportunity to take part in an 'Attention and Listening in the Early Years' group on a regular basis, children learn from joining in with adapted songs and listening activities which might require them to:

- wait to take a turn
- respond to their name or to the name of an object they're holding
- match a sound to an object/animal
- match their responses (shaking an instrument or singing, for instance) to different speeds ('This little train goes up the hill') or volumes ('I hear thunder') in a song
- stop when the music stops, or when they hear the word 'Stop'
- perform a specific action on the word 'Go' in a 'Ready, steady, go' game.

By means of such activities, we can develop a child's ability to attend and listen to its full potential.

How to run an 'Attention and Listening in the Early Years' group

To run the group you will need to consider the following.

Venue and setting

If you already have a circle time during an Early Years session, this is an ideal time to run your group. All the children settle down together, and so there are fewer visual distractions (e.g. people moving around) and auditory distractions (e.g. background noise). If this also follows a tidy-up time, this would mean even fewer distractions, i.e. because no toys which aren't being used in the group, are in sight. The children need to be comfortable, whether this means on cushions on the floor or on appropriate chairs. We all know how difficult it is to concentrate when we're uncomfortable. If parents are involved in your setting, be sure to encourage their involvement in the group, as this gives a good model for the children and encourages the parents to feel more confident about trying some of the ideas at home.

Time allocation

Each group session should run for no longer than 15 to 25 minutes, depending on the ages and/or developmental levels of the children. If the group goes on for too long, you will not be able to hold the children's attention, and will risk reducing the benefit gained.

Ideally the group should run weekly at least, daily at most, for the same group of children, for them to get maximum benefit. If you run the group weekly and, in your setting, you have different children attending on different days of the week, don't run the group on different days each week. Run it on the same day so that a specific group can be included, then, after about ten weeks (or a term), run the group on a different day so that a new group of children can benefit.

Resources

Each group is run following a theme such as 'The Farm' (see pages 70–88) or 'The Zoo' (see pages 105–122), and appropriate visual props, toy animals for instance, are needed (see suggested plans). It is recommended that for each theme the appropriate props be kept specifically for use when running the group, in appropriately themed and labelled bags, for example, to reduce the time and effort needed to prepare for running a group. Keep the ready-made plans at the end of this manual, or your own plans, also in the themed bags.

You will also require a Listening Box in which to keep the resources for the current group session, and in particular for the 'What's in the Listening Box today?' activity (see page 19). This needs to be a lidded container, which is large enough to hold all of the resources for one session.

It is useful to keep any instruments that you might need for the group in a separate container of their own, a cloth bag for instance. This makes the giving out and collecting of the instruments run much more smoothly and quickly, and so reduces the likelihood of losing the children's attention.

Most important, you will need the star of your show, a puppet. A puppet with big ears is recommended, so as to press home to the children that the group is about listening. When the author originally ran this group, a lop-eared rabbit puppet called 'Lucy' was used, but anything with large ears would serve equally well.

How to help the children to listen, attend and join in

- Give the puppet a name and then use it to introduce the aim of listening (hence its big ears). Keep the puppet involved throughout the group – children often attend to a puppet better than to an adult!
- Use the same general format for every group (see next chapter). Familiarization helps the children understand what is required, so that they are more likely to join in and gain benefit as a result.
- To support an individual child's ability to listen, get his/her attention by saying his/her name and then waiting for a response, such as stilling or eye contact, before continuing.
- Before each activity, talk children through what will be expected of them; for instance: 'In the next song (see 'Five little ducks go swimming along' song and activity p.65), listen out for your name and if you hear it, put your duck on the pond.' All children learn best by being shown what to do, so use the props/toys that the child will be using, to demonstrate beforehand, and/or get a colleague to take the first turn in an activity, so as to model for the children what is expected of them.
- Praise the children, individually or as a group, for good listening. Make sure it is clear to the children what you mean by 'good listening'; for instance: 'Well done, Adam, you're looking at me/sitting still/not talking. That's good listening!'
- Keep your language simple enough for the ages/stages of development of the children in the group. Children will soon lose interest and therefore concentration if the language is hard to understand. Poor

attention skills can be a first sign of immature language skills; if in doubt, simplify your language.

- Use visual cues, such as gesture, pointing and mime, and props such as toys and puppets, to help the children attend and understand what you are saying and what you want them to do. Increase the visual cues if a child seems to be struggling to attend, understand and/or join in, or if any of the children have hearing difficulties.
- Use good communication skills yourself. Make sure your voice is loud enough, your words are clearly spoken, and that you use 'good listening skills'. Use intonation and make your voice interesting enough for the children to want to listen; if you sound interested in what is going on, or excited at the appropriate moments, the children will become interested and excited too.
- Keep the numbers of children in the group manageable – too many children will distract each other. Around ten children in a group is manageable if none of the children have severe attention problems, and as long as you have enough space for them all to sit comfortably. Fewer than six children is recommended if the children have been selected for the group because of particular need for work on their attention and listening skills.
- Encourage all the children to start a song at the same time; count them in if necessary – for instance: '1, 2, 3...Twinkle, twinkle, little star...'
- Don't rush the songs or activities. Children take longer than adults to take in information, and to respond, so they are more likely to learn from a song or activity if they are allowed to take their time over it.
- Don't be afraid to repeat songs and activities within a group session. You could even repeat a whole theme for a few successive sessions. In fact this type of repetition is very important, as children love the familiarity of repetition, and it helps them to understand and learn. However, it is also important to change your theme regularly, and not use the same one more than about six times in succession, otherwise, if children become too familiar with the songs and activities and no longer need to put any effort into attending and listening, they are no longer learning skills in these areas.
- Don't worry if the children don't attend and join in as well as you think they should in the first few sessions. They may need time to get used to the group and what is expected of them. Keeping to the same format each time, as suggested in this manual, will assist this process.

- Very important is to keep it fun! We all learn best when we're enjoying ourselves, and children are no exception.

Themes, activities and songs

Each 'Attention and Listening in the Early Years' group session is planned around a theme, providing an anchor for the children to gain meaning from the activities and songs, helping them build their understanding of the world around them, and strengthening the related vocabulary and their language skills generally. The group is presented as a short, simple story within the theme, using the activities and songs to lend illustration to, and experience of, the story.

The general format of a group stays the same each time, so the children quickly familiarize themselves with what is expected of them and so are more able to join in. Children learn better in a routine that provides a secure and familiar environment. The general format is:

1. Hello song (see page 16).
2. Introduction of the theme via a song, 'What's in the Listening Box today?' (see page 16 and page 19), and the Listening Box activity. The latter involves guessing the contents of the box from sounds (listening) and/or mimes (looking), and so begins to facilitate the children's listening and attention skills.
3. Story, listening activities and adapted songs appropriate to the theme.
4. The song 'Twinkle, twinkle, little star' to signal the end of the story and to help the children settle down.
5. Goodbye song (see page 16).

The songs included in this format are:

HELLO SONG
(to the tune of 'Nice one, Cyril')

Hello X [puppet's name], hello X,

Hello everyone,

It's nice to see you here.

'WHAT'S IN THE LISTENING BOX TODAY?'
(to the tune of 'What shall we do with the drunken sailor?')

What's in the Listening Box today?

What's in the Listening Box today?

What's in the Listening Box today?

What's in the Listening Box?

GOODBYE SONG
(to the tune of 'Nice one, Cyril')

Goodbye X [puppet's name], goodbye X,

Goodbye everyone,

We'll see you all next time/week.

Sample themes and plans

What follows is six sample themes for you to design your 'Attention and Listening in the Early Years' group around, with suggested plans (for photocopying) and some further alternative songs and activities which might be included with those themes. The list is by no means exhaustive; many of you who have experience working with young children will have plenty of ideas about themes, activities and songs which could also be adapted for use – for instance, designing the theme around a recent playschool trip, or around the general class theme of the term (e.g. the seaside, healthy eating, or transport).

For each theme, there are two versions of the same plan. Version 1 is more detailed, in order that you have enough information on how to run the session most effectively; this is for you to use when you are going through the session by way of preparation beforehand. Version 2 is a shorter version, which you can keep by your side during the session as a prompt.

1. A Day at Home (Version 1)

Resources

Into the Listening Box, put:

- brush
- toothbrush
- key
- flannel or sponge
- cup and spoon.

You will also need:

- claves (percussion sticks) and shakers
- feely bag of toy or real items of food of very different shapes and textures, e.g. apple, banana, biscuit, carrot, cauliflower
- large plate.

Starter activitiy

Introduce your puppet, why you are all here and what you mean by 'good listening'. For example: *'Hello, this is X* [puppet's name]. *Can you see his/her big ears? That's so he/she can be a "good listener". We're all going to do some "good listening" with X today. "Good listening" is:*

- ☐ *not talking*
- ☐ *sitting still*
- ☐ *looking at who is talking*
- ☐ *thinking about the words.*

Well done, [child's name], *you are sitting still – that's "good listening"!'*

Throughout the group session, regularly prompt for good listening, i.e. look out for children exhibiting 'good listening' skills and praise them in this way as a positive method of reminding the whole group what is expected of them. It is harder to tell if a child is 'thinking about the words', but praise them for this if, for example, they lift up the object they are holding at the appropriate moment in 'Guess the mime' on page 21.

HELLO SONG

Lesson objectives: **To signal the beginning of the group session, gaining the children's attention and interest for taking part in the following activities.**

Main activity

Say: *'Let's all sing "hello" to X* [puppet's name], *and make him/her feel welcome.'*

Hello X, hello X,

Hello everyone,

It's nice to see you here.

- Prompt for 'good listening'.

'WHAT'S IN THE LISTENING BOX TODAY?' SONG AND ACTIVITY

Lesson objectives **Listening for and/or looking at clues to the contents of the box. Also introduces the theme for the session.**

Main activity

Encourage the children to clap as you sing the song to get their attention and get them involved even before they have learned the words.

Say: 'X [puppet's name] *has brought along his/her Listening Box. I wonder what's in it today? Let's clap along to the song.'*

What's in the Listening Box today?

What's in the Listening Box today?

What's in the Listening Box today?

What's in the Listening Box?

After the song, keep the children's attention by making a big thing about there being something hidden in the Listening Box. Tell them that you are going to mime something that is in the box and they have to guess what it is. Mime one of the objects (e.g. 'brush' your hair/'clean' your teeth/'lock' a door/'wash' your face/'stir' your tea) and say: *'What do you think I'm doing...so what do we use to do that/what is in the box?'*

NB: This Listening Box activity involves *looking* rather than *listening*, so developing the children's visual, rather than auditory, attention skills.

If a child guesses correctly, bring the object out of the box and mime it again to match the mime to the object, particularly for those who have not yet understood/made the connection. If none of the children guesses the object correctly, mime the object again. If they still have not guessed after seeing the mime twice, do it again and at the same time bring the object briefly out of the box to give the children a visual prompt. If the children are still unable to guess the name of the object, show them, say its name and mime it again to help the children to learn.

- Repeat for four to six different (or repeated) objects in the Listening Box – no more than this or you may lose the children's attention.
- To avoid distracting the children from the main activity, wait until you have finished the Listening Box activity before giving out an object to each child and keeping a set for yourself, for demonstration purposes. So that they attend and listen to the introduction to the next activity, tell them to leave their object on the floor in front of them until you say that they can pick them up.
- Once the objects are given out, make sure the children have understood what the theme for the session is by summarizing as follows: *'So where do you think we are today, somewhere you can see all these things?* [Pause to give the children a chance to guess.] *Today we are at home with X* [puppet's name].'
- Prompt for 'good listening'. Praise anyone who, for example, is *'...looking at me – well done, that's "good listening".'*

GUESS THE MIME ACTIVITY

Lesson objectives   Matching a mime to an object held in a child's hand.

Main activity

Tell the children that they can pick up their objects and that you are going to pretend to use one of them, and they are to guess which one by holding it up for everyone to see. Prepare them for this by saying: 'So *if I do this* [pretend to stir a cup of tea] *I am pretending to stir my tea: who has the cup and spoon? Hold them up in the air.'*

Then mime all the activities one by one, i.e. cleaning teeth/washing face, etc., and allow the children to guess what it is, demonstrating their awareness by holding up the object that goes with it. It is good practice, if you have enough of each object, to have one of each type yourself to hold up and give the children an extra, visual prompt (if they need it) as to which object is being mimed, whether it is the same object as the one they have and what to do if it is.

'THIS IS THE WAY WE...' SONG AND ACTIVITY

Lesson objectives **Matching an object to its name sung in a song.**

Main activity

Tell the children that you are all going to sing a song about the things we do at home, and that they are to watch and listen for their object and hold it up in the air, as before. You can demonstrate again, if you think the children need that extra support. Then sing the song, encouraging the children to hold up the object appropriate to each new verse. It helps if you use your own set of objects to demonstrate as you sing. You can also encourage the children who don't have the object being sung about in a particular verse to mime the action instead.

(to the tune of 'Here we go round the mulberry bush')

This is the way we clean our teeth,
Clean our teeth, clean our teeth,
This is the way we clean our teeth,
On a cold and frosty morning.
This is the way we wash our face, etc.
This is the way we brush our hair, etc.
This is the way we stir the tea, etc.
This is the way we *unlock the cupboard*, etc.

- Link to the next activity. Say: *'Okay, now we've unlocked the cupboard where we keep the food, let's get it out and chop up some food for dinner.'*
- Put away the cups, flannels, keys, etc., give out the claves (telling the children to leave them on the floor in front of them until you say that they can pick them up) and have the feely bag of food ready for the next activity.
- Prompt for 'good listening'. Praise anyone who, for example, is *'...not talking – well done, that's "good listening".'*

'CHOP, CHOP' SONG AND ACTIVITY

Lesson objectives **Tactile (touch)-focused attention to an item in a feely bag.**

Main activity

Say to the children: *'In this bag I've got the food that needs chopping. Let's see if you can guess what food we are going to chop, by feeling in this bag.'*

If possible, get another adult to do this first, to demonstrate what is needed. The adult puts their hand in the bag and guesses what they are touching before pulling the item out. Then you all sing the song (using the claves to make a chopping sound), with the person who pulled out the food pretending to chop it with their hand. Then some of the children have a turn, with support of an adult as necessary.

(to the tune of 'Skip to my Lou')

Chop, chop, chop up the lot,

Chop, chop, chop up the lot,
Chop, chop, chop up the lot,

Chop it all up for dinner.

- Repeat, giving about five different children a turn. (No more, or you may lose their attention.)
- Put away the claves and give out an item of food to each child, keeping a set of all the different foods for yourself, for demonstration purposes.
- Place a large plate in the middle of the circle.
- Prompt for 'good listening'. Praise anyone who, for example, is '*...sitting still – well done, that's "good listening".*'

'LET'S ALL HAVE SOME DINNER' SONG AND ACTIVITY

Lesson objectives **Listening for, then responding to, the name of a specific food.**

Main activity

Make sure each child knows the item of food that they are holding, then say: *'Listen out for the name of the food you are holding, in the song, and if you hear its name, put it on the plate.'*

Demonstrate: *'So if we sing about "apple", who's got an apple? Put it on the plate like this.'*

NB: To encourage good listening, ensure that the children sit down again as soon as they have placed an item of food on the plate. Also, please note that the first verse is an introduction only; no food is placed on the plate during this verse.

Let's all have some dinner, some dinner, some dinner.
Let's all have some dinner,
Some dinner for you and me.
Let's all have some *apple*, some apple, some apple.
Let's all have some apple,
Some apple for you and me.

Let's all have a *banana*, banana, banana...[etc.]
Let's all have a *carrot*, a carrot, a carrot...[etc.]

- Put away the food and plate.
- Prompt for 'good listening'.
- Give out the shakers, telling the children to leave them on the floor until you tell them to pick them up. Make sure that you and your colleagues have a shaker each as well, but leave yours on the floor as a good model for the children.

'SHAKE 'N' SHAKE' SONG AND ACTIVITY

Lesson objectives Listening for and responding to the word 'Stop'.

Main activity

Say: *'So we've had some dinner, now let's have some fun. Let's sing a shaky song.'* Tell the children to listen out for the word 'Stop' in the song. Say: *'When you hear the word "Stop"* [put your hand up in a "stop" gesture as an extra, visual prompt], *stop shaking your shaker.'*

(to the tune of 'Here we go round the mulberry bush')

Shake and shake and shake and shake,

Shake and shake, shake and shake,

Shake and shake and shake and STOP. [*Put hand up in 'STOP' gesture.*]

Shake and shake and shake.

Let's go up, let's go down, in the air, on the ground,
Shake it, shake it all around.

In your lap, shhh [*index finger to lips as a visual prompt*], don't make a sound.

- Collect all the shakers and put them away to reduce any distraction.
- Prompt for 'good listening'.

SONG: 'TWINKLE, TWINKLE, LITTLE STAR'

Lesson objectives **Settling the children down at the end of what may have been an exciting session for them.**

Main activity

Say: *'It's late now, time for the stars to come out and for us to rest. Here are my stars.* [Hold up your fingers and twinkle them like stars.] *Has anybody else got any stars?'* [Encourage the children to do the same.]

Twinkle, twinkle, little star,

How I wonder what you are,

Up above the world so high,

Like a diamond in the sky.

Twinkle, twinkle, little star,

How I wonder what you are.

GOODBYE SONG

Lesson objectives **To signal the end of the group session.**

Main activity

Say: *'And now it's time for X* [puppet's name] *to go home, so let's sing goodbye to him/her.'*

Goodbye X, goodbye X,

Goodbye everyone,

We'll see you all next time.

A Day at Home (Version 2)

Resources

Into the Listening Box, put:

- brush
- toothbrush
- key
- flannel or sponge
- cup and spoon.

You will also need:

- claves and shakers
- feely bag of toy or real foods of very different shapes and textures
- large plate.

Starter activity

Say: *'Hello, this is X* [puppet's name]. *Can you see his/her big ears? That's so he/she can be a "good listener". We're all going to do some "good listening" with X today. "Good listening" is:*

☐ *not talking*

☐ *sitting still*

☐ *looking at who is talking*

☐ *thinking about the words.*

Well done, Y [child's name], *you are sitting still – that's "good listening"!'*

HELLO SONG

Main activity

Say: *'Let's all sing "hello" to X* [puppet's name], *and make him/her feel welcome.'*

> Hello X, hello X,
>
> Hello everyone,
>
> It's nice to see you here.

- Prompt for 'good listening'.

'WHAT'S IN THE LISTENING BOX TODAY?' SONG AND ACTIVITY

Main activity

Say: *'X* [puppet's name] *has brought along his/her Listening Box. I wonder what's in it today? Let's clap along to the song.'*

> What's in the Listening Box today?
>
> What's in the Listening Box today?
>
> What's in the Listening Box today?
>
> What's in the Listening Box?

Then say: *'I am going to mime/pretend to use something in this box – try to guess what it is I am doing.'* As you mime each one, say: *'What do you think I am doing?... So what do we use to do that? That's right, I was stirring my tea, with a cup and spoon.'*

- Give out one object to each child but keep a set for yourself, for demonstration purposes.

Say: *'Leave them on the floor until I say.'*

Also: *'So where do you think we are today, somewhere you can see all these things?... Today we are staying at home with X* [puppet's name].*'*

- Prompt for 'good listening'.

GUESS THE MIME ACTIVITY

Main activity

Say: *'Pick up your objects. I am going to pretend to use one of the objects, see if you can guess which one, then hold it up for everyone to see.'* Prepare them for this by saying: *'So if I do this* [pretend to stir a cup of tea] *I am pretending to stir my tea. Who has the cup and spoon? Hold them up in the air.'*

- Repeat for all objects.
- Prompt for 'good listening'.

'THIS IS THE WAY WE...' SONG AND ACTIVITY

Main activity

Say: *'Now we are all going to sing a song about the things we do at home; watch and listen for your object and hold it up in the air, if we sing about it. See if you can do all the actions as we sing the words too.'*

(to the tune of 'Here we go round the mulberry bush')

This is the way we clean our teeth,
Clean our teeth, clean our teeth,
This is the way we clean our teeth,
On a cold and frosty morning.

This is the way we wash our face, etc.
This is the way we brush our hair, etc.
This is the way we unlock the cupboard, etc.
This is the way we stir the tea, etc.

- Link to the next activity. Say: *'Okay, now we've unlocked the cupboard where we keep the food, let's get it out and chop up some food for dinner.'*
- Put away the cups, flannels, keys, etc., give out the claves and have the feely bag of food ready. Say: *'Leave the claves on the floor until I say that you can pick them up.'*
- Prompt for 'good listening'.

'CHOP, CHOP' SONG AND ACTIVITY

Main activity

Say: *'In this bag I've got the food that needs chopping. Let's see if you can guess what food we are going to chop by feeling in this bag.'*

An adult demonstrates, then five children (at most, so that you don't lose their attention) take a turn to feel in the bag and guess what the item of food is. Everyone sings the song below (using the claves to make a chopping sound), with the person who pulled out the food pretending to chop it with their hand.

(to the tune of 'Skip to my Lou')

Chop, chop, chop up the lot,

Chop, chop, chop up the lot,

Chop, chop, chop up the lot,

Chop it all up for dinner.

- Repeat about five times.
- Put away the claves and give out an item of food to each child.
- Place a large plate in the middle of the circle.
- Prompt for 'good listening'.

'LET'S ALL HAVE SOME DINNER' SONG AND ACTIVITY

Main activity

Say: *'Listen out for the name of the food you are holding, in the song, and if you hear its name, put it on the plate.'* Demonstrate: *'So if we sing about "apple", who's got an apple? Put it on the plate.'*

Let's all have some dinner, some dinner, some dinner.
Let's all have some dinner,
Some dinner for you and me.

Let's all have some apple, some apple, some apple.
Let's all have some apple,
Some apple for you and me.

Let's all have a *banana*, banana, banana... [etc.]
Let's all have a *carrot*, a carrot, a carrot... [etc.]

- Put away the food and plate.
- Prompt for 'good listening'.
- Give out the shakers.

'SHAKE 'N' SHAKE' SONG AND ACTIVITY

Main activity

Say: *'So we've had some dinner, now let's have some fun. Let's sing a shaky song. Listen out for the word "Stop"* [add visual clue], *and stop shaking your shaker when you hear it.'*

(to the tune of 'Here we go round the mulberry bush')

Shake and shake and shake and shake,

Shake and shake, shake and shake,

Shake and shake and shake and STOP. [*Put hand up in 'STOP' gesture.*]
Shake and shake and shake.

Let's go up, let's go down, in the air, on the ground,

Shake it, shake it all around.

In your lap, shhh[*index finger as a visual prompt*], don't make a sound.

- Collect shakers and put them away.
- Prompt for 'good listening'.

SONG: 'TWINKLE, TWINKLE, LITTLE STAR'

Main activity

Say: *'It's late now, time for the stars to come out and for us to rest. Here are my stars, has anybody else got any stars?'*

Twinkle, twinkle, little star,

How I wonder what you are,

Up above the world so high,

Like a diamond in the sky.

Twinkle, twinkle, little star,

How I wonder what you are.

GOODBYE SONG

Main activity

Say: *'Now it's time for X* [puppet's name] *to go home, so let's sing goodbye to him/her.'*

Goodbye X, goodbye X,

Goodbye everyone,

We'll see you all next time.

A Day at Home – further ideas

MATCH THE MUSIC ACTIVITY

Give each child a pair of instruments, ensuring that the instruments have very different sounds, e.g. a bell and a drum. Make a sound with one from your own pair of hidden instruments and ask the children to play the one that matches. (Children need to be prepared beforehand by having the chance to match instrument to instrument while yours are still in view.)

'OLD MACDONALD HAD A HOUSE' SONG AND ACTIVITY

In this activity, children hold the prop (e.g. a toy or picture of keys, telephone, clock, door) up in the air when they hear its name.

Old MacDonald had a house,

E–I–E–I–O,

And in that house he had some *keys (telephone/clock/door)*

E–I–E–I–O,

With a *jingle jangle (ring, ring/tick, tock/creak, creak)* here

And a jingle jangle there, here a jingle, there a jangle,

Everywhere a jingle jangle… [etc.]

WHAT'S IN THE WASH BAG? ACTIVITY

Resources

- cloth 'washing bag'
- items of clothing
- cardboard box 'washing machine'.

Say: *'Let's help X* [puppet's name] *do the washing.'*

One item is put secretly into the bag at a time, then children take it in turns to feel the object and try to guess what it is. Make it easier by having very different items (e.g. a shoe or a belt) or very different materials (e.g. a woolly jumper or a T-shirt). Children may need a clue, e.g. 'You wear it on your foot.' Children then put each item into the washing machine to complete the game.

'THIS IS THE WAY WE...' SONG AND ACTIVITY

(to the tune of 'What shall we do with the drunken sailor?')

This is the way we sort the clothes,

This is the way we sort the clothes,

This is the way we sort the clothes,

Early in the morning.

You could also sing verses for:

- wash the clothes/switch on the machine
- hang up the clothes
- iron the clothes... Early in the morning.

In this game, everyone mimes the actions as you sing. Children have to watch and listen carefully to join in.

WHO'S WEARING WHAT? ACTIVITY

A game in which the children need to listen for the name of an item of clothing, then think about whether or not it is something they are wearing, and, if so, (for example) jumping into the middle of the circle.

- Say: *'If you're wearing socks, jump into the middle of the circle,'* etc.
- Repeat, so that all children get to hear the name of an item of clothing they are wearing before jumping into the circle.

2. A Musical Day Out (Version 1)

Resources

Into the Listening Box, put:

- shakers
- bells
- claves.

You will also need:

- toy food
- plate
- small kites (kite shapes cut from coloured paper with a ribbon as a tail).

Starter activity

Introduce your puppet, why you are all here and what you mean by 'good listening'. For example: '*Hello, this is X* [puppet's name]. *Can you see his/her big ears? That's so he/she can be a "good listener". We're all going to do some "good listening" with X today. "Good listening" is:*

☐ *not talking*

☐ *sitting still*

☐ *looking at who is talking*

☐ *thinking about the words.*

Well done Y, [child's name], *you are sitting still – that's "good listening"!*'
Throughout the group session you should look out for children exhibiting 'good listening' skills and praise them in this way as a positive method of reminding the whole group what is expected of them. It is harder to tell if a child is 'thinking about the words', but praise them for this if, for example, they put the right piece of food on the plate during the 'Let's all have a picnic' song and activity on page 41.

HELLO SONG

Lesson objectives **To signal the beginning of the group session, gaining the children's attention and interest for taking part in the following activities.**

Main activity

Say: *'Let's all sing "hello" to X* [puppet's name], *and make him/her feel welcome.'*

> Hello X, hello X,
>
> Hello everyone,
>
> It's nice to see you here.

- Prompt for 'good listening'. Praise anyone who, for example, is *'...looking at me – well done, that's "good listening".'*

'WHAT'S IN THE LISTENING BOX TODAY?' SONG AND ACTIVITY

Lesson objectives **Listening and/or looking at clues to the contents of the box. (The activity also introduces the theme for the session.)**

Main activity

Encourage them to clap as you sing the song, to get their attention and get them involved even before they have learned the words. Say: 'X [puppet's name] *has brought along his/her Listening Box. I wonder what's* in it today? Let's clap along to the song.'

> What's in the Listening Box today?
>
> What's in the Listening Box today?

What's in the Listening Box today?

What's in the Listening Box?

After the song, keep the children's attention by making a big thing about what you've got hidden in the Listening Box. Tell them that you are going to make a noise with something in the box and they have to guess what it is. Play one of the instruments out of sight of the children (maybe using the lid of the box as a barrier) and say: *'What do you think it is?'*

If a child guesses correctly, bring the instrument out of the box and play it again to match the sound to the instrument, particularly for those who have not yet understood/made the connection. If none of the children guesses the instrument correctly, play it again. If they still have not guessed after hearing it twice, play the instrument again and at the same time bring it briefly out of the box to give the children a visual prompt. If the children are still unable to guess the name of the instrument, show it to them, say its name and play it again to help the children to learn.

- Repeat for four to six different (or some repeated) instruments in the Listening Box – no more than this, or you may lose the children's attention. Also be careful not to use too many different types of instruments – two or three is sufficient – so as not to make the activity too complex for the children and lose their attention.

- To avoid distracting the children from the main activity, wait until you have finished the Listening Box activity before giving out an instrument to each child and keeping a full set for yourself, for demonstration purposes. So that they attend and listen to the introduction to the next activity, tell them to leave their instruments on the floor in front of them until you say that they can pick them up.

- Make sure the children know what the theme for the session is by summarizing as follows: *'Today we are going on a musical day out with X [puppet's name].'*

- Prompt for 'good listening'. Tell the children to 'listen'. Praise anyone who, for example, is *'...not talking – well done, that's "good listening".'*

'THIS LITTLE TRAIN GOES UP THE HILL' SONG AND ACTIVITY

Lesson objectives **Listening for and responding to a change of rate in a song.**

Main activity

Tell the children to pick up their instruments. Say: 'X [puppet's name] *is taking us on a train. The train has got to get up a hill, so at first it goes very slowly.'* Demonstrate playing an instrument slowly and encourage the children to do the same. *'Then it goes a bit faster.'* Demonstrate. *'Then it goes very fast, it goes racing down the hill.'* Demonstrate.

(to the tune of 'What shall we do with the drunken sailor?')

This little train goes up the hill,
This little train goes up the hill,
This little train goes up the hill,
This little train goes slowly.

This little train goes along the top, etc.
...This little train goes faster.

This little train goes down the hill, etc.
...This little train goes racing.

- Put the instruments away temporarily.
- Prompt for 'good listening'. Praise anyone who, for example, is '*...sitting still – well done, that's "good listening".*'

'KITES FLY WAY UP HIGH' SONG AND ACTIVITY

Lesson objectives **Looking, listening and responding to 'up' and 'down' actions during a song.**

Main activity

Say: *'We're here! We've come to a big green hill and children are at the top, flying their kites high up in the sky.'*

Give out the kites and tell the children to leave them on the floor until you tell them to pick them up.

Say: *'Listen and watch for when the kites go up* [demonstrate] *and down* [demonstrate] *in the song, and make your kites do the same. Now pick up your kites.'*

(to the tune of 'Row, row, row your boat')

Kites fly way up high, climbing in the sky.

Breeze is dropping, kites are flopping

Down onto the ground.

Up, down, up, down.

(Then repeat 'up' and 'down' randomly a few more times, to really challenge the children to keep looking, listening and moving their kites accordingly.)

NB: The children may try to stand up during this activity; encourage them to stay sitting down and just move their kites up and down, or else you may lose their attention.

- Put the kites away.
- Prompt for 'good listening'.

'LET'S ALL HAVE A PICNIC' SONG AND ACTIVITY

Lesson objectives **Listening for and responding to the name of an item of food.**

Main activity

Have the food ready and put the plate in the middle of the circle.

Say: *'It's time for a picnic. X* [puppet's name] *has brought some food. You can each have some but leave it on the floor until I say to pick it up.'*

The children are each given a piece of food and the group leader makes sure they know the name of the food. Say: *'Listen for the name of your food in the song, then come and put it on the plate,'* then demonstrate this for the children by saying, *'So if we sing about pizza and you are holding a piece of pizza, put it on the plate like this.'*
NB: the first verse is an introduction only – no food is placed on the plate at this stage.

> Let's all have a picnic, a picnic, a picnic.
> Let's all have a picnic,
> A picnic for you and me.
>
> Let's all have some *pizza*, some pizza, some pizza.
> Let's all have some pizza,
> Some pizza for you and me...etc. [to include all the food names]

NB: 1. Don't have more than about five different types of food, or the song will be so long that you will lose the children's interest.

2. Ensure that the children sit down again as soon as they have placed an item of food on the plate.

- After the activity put away the food and plate.
- Give out the shakers and bells but tell the children to leave them on the floor until you tell them to pick them up. Make sure that you and your colleagues have an instrument each too, but leave yours on the floor as a good model for the children.
- Prompt for 'good listening'.

'I HEAR THUNDER' SONG AND ACTIVITY

Lesson objectives **Listening to the difference between 'noisy' and 'quiet' sounds and joining in accordingly.**

Main activity

Explain to the children that it is now raining and thundering on the hill. Ask them to listen to the rain while you make a quiet sound with your shaker. Then ask them to listen to the thunder while you make a loud sound with your shaker. Say: *'Uh-oh, the weather is getting bad. Can you hear the thunder? It's very loud* [demonstrate with instruments]. *And the rain, it's very quiet* [demonstrate].*'* Then tell the children to pick up their shakers and join in as you make a quiet 'rain' sound and a noisy 'thunder' sound. Tell them that you are all going to sing a song in which there will be rain and thunder, and they are to make quiet and noisy sounds with their shakers along with the song.

(to the tune of 'Frère Jacques')

I hear thunder, I hear thunder [loudly with instruments].

Hark! Don't you? Hark! Don't you?

Pitter patter raindrops, pitter patter raindrops [quietly with instruments].

I'm wet through! So are you!

- Prompt for 'good listening'.

'SHAKE 'N' SHAKE' SONG AND ACTIVITY

Lesson objectives   Listening for and responding to the word 'Stop'.

Main activity

Say: *'After all that rain we're wet and cold – let's sing a shaky song to warm us up!'* Tell the children to listen out for the word 'Stop' in the song. Say: *'When you hear the word "Stop"* [put your hand up in a "stop" gesture as an extra, visual prompt], *stop shaking your shaker.'*

(to the tune of 'Here we go round the mulberry bush')

Shake and shake and shake and shake,

Shake and shake, shake and shake,

Shake and shake and shake and STOP [*visual prompt*].

Shake and shake and shake.
Let's go up, let's go down, in the air, on the ground,

Shake it, shake it all around.

In your lap, shhh [*index finger to lips as a visual prompt*], don't make a sound.

- Collect all the shakers and put them away to reduce any distraction.
- Prompt for 'good listening'.

SONG: 'TWINKLE, TWINKLE, CHOCOLATE BAR'

Lesson objectives **Settling the children down at the end of what may have been an exciting session for them.**

Main activity

Say: *'It's time to go home now and X's dad has come to give us a lift in his rusty car.'*

Twinkle, twinkle, chocolate bar,

Your dad drives a rusty car.

Press the starter, pull the choke,

Off he goes in a cloud of smoke.

Twinkle, twinkle, chocolate bar,

Your dad drives a rusty car.

GOODBYE SONG

Lesson objectives **To signal the end of the group session.**

Main activity

Say: *'And now let's sing goodbye to X* [puppet's name].*'*

Goodbye X, goodbye X,

Goodbye everyone,

We'll see you all next time.

A Musical Day Out (Version 2)

Resources

Into the Listening Box, put:

- shakers
- bells
- claves.

You will also need:

- toy food
- plate
- small kites.

Starter activity

Say: *'Hello, this is X* [puppet's name]. *Can you see his/her big ears? That's so he/she can be a "good listener". We're all going to do some "good listening" with X today. "Good listening" is:*

- ☐ *not talking*
- ☐ *sitting still*
- ☐ *looking at who is talking*
- ☐ *thinking about the words.*

Well done, Y [child's name], *you are sitting still – that's "good listening"!'*

HELLO SONG

Main activity

Say: *'Let's all sing "hello" to X* [puppet's name], *and make him/her feel welcome.'*

Hello X, hello X,

Hello everyone,

It's nice to see you here.

- Prompt for 'good listening'.

'WHAT'S IN THE LISTENING BOX TODAY?' SONG AND ACTIVITY

Main activity

Say: *'Let's clap along to the song'* [demonstrate].

What's in the Listening Box today?

What's in the Listening Box today?

What's in the Listening Box today?

What's in the Listening Box?

Play one of the instruments, keeping it hidden, and say: *'What do you think it is?'* If a child guesses correctly, bring the instrument out of the box.

- Give out all of the instruments but keep a set for yourself, for demonstration purposes.

To ensure that the children understand what the theme of the session is, say: *'So today X* [puppet's name] *is taking us on a musical day out!'*

- Prompt for 'good listening'.

'THIS LITTLE TRAIN GOES UP THE HILL' SONG AND ACTIVITY

Main activity

Say: *'Pick up your instruments.* X [puppet's name] *is taking us on a train. The train has got to get up a hill, so at first it goes very slowly.'* [Demonstrate.] *'Then it goes a bit faster.'* [Demonstrate.] *'Then it goes very fast, it goes racing down the hill.'* [Demonstrate.]

(to the tune of 'What shall we do with the drunken sailor?')

This little train goes up the hill,
This little train goes up the hill,
This little train goes up the hill,
This little train goes slowly.

This little train goes along the top, etc.
...This little train goes faster.

This little train goes down the hill, etc.
...This little train goes racing.

- Prompt for 'good listening'.
- Say: *'We're here! We've come to a big green hill and children are at the top flying their kites high up in the sky.'*

'KITES FLY WAY UP HIGH' SONG AND ACTIVITY

Main activity

Say: *'Listen and watch for when the kites go up* [demonstrate] *and down* [demonstrate].*'*

> (to the tune of 'Row, row, row your boat')
>
> Kites fly way up high, climbing in the sky.
>
> Breeze is dropping, kites are flopping
> Down onto the ground.
>
> Up, down, up, down.
>
> (Repeat 'up' and 'down' randomly.)

- Put away the kites; bring out the toy food and plate.
- Prompt for 'good listening'.

'LET'S ALL HAVE A PICNIC' SONG AND ACTIVITY

Main activity

Have the food ready and put the plate in the middle of the circle.

Say: *'It's time for a picnic. X* [puppet's name] *has brought some food. You can each have a piece but leave it on the floor until I say to pick it up.'* Give out the food and say: *'Listen for the name of your food in the song, then come and put it on the plate.'* [Demonstrate.]

> Let's all have a picnic, a picnic, a picnic.
> Let's all have a picnic,
> A picnic for you and me.
>
> Let's all have some *pizza*, some pizza, some pizza.
> Let's all have some pizza,
> Some pizza for you and me... [etc.]

- Put food and plate away; give out shakers and bells and say: *'Leave them on the floor until I say to pick them up.'*
- Prompt for 'good listening'.

'I HEAR THUNDER' SONG AND ACTIVITY

Main activity

Say: *'Uh-oh, the weather is getting bad. Can you hear the thunder? It's very loud* [demonstrate with instruments]. *And the rain, it's very quiet* [demonstrate].'

(to the tune of 'Frère Jacques')

I hear thunder, I hear thunder [*loudly with instruments*].

Hark! Don't you? Hark! Don't you?

Pitter patter raindrops, pitter patter raindrops [*quietly with instruments*]

I'm wet through! So are you!

- Prompt for 'good listening'.

'SHAKE 'N' SHAKE' SONG AND ACTIVITY

Main activity

Say: *'After all that rain we're cold and wet – let's sing a shaky song to warm us up. Listen out for the "Stop"* [add visual clue], *and stop shaking your instrument when you hear it.'*

(to the tune of 'Here we go round the mulberry bush')

Shake and shake and shake and shake,

Shake and shake, shake and shake,

Shake and shake and shake and STOP [*visual prompt*].

Shake and shake and shake.
Let's go up, let's go down, in the air, on the ground,

Shake it, shake it all around.

In your lap, shhh [*visual prompt*], don't make a sound.

- Collect all the shakers and put them away.
- Prompt for 'good listening'.

SONG: 'TWINKLE, TWINKLE, CHOCOLATE BAR'

Main activity

Say: *'It's time to go home and X's dad has come to give us a lift in his rusty car.'*

Twinkle, twinkle, chocolate bar,

Your dad drives a rusty car.

Press the starter, pull the choke,

Off he goes in a cloud of smoke.

Twinkle, twinkle, chocolate bar,

Your dad drives a rusty car.

GOODBYE SONG

Main activity

Say: *'And now let's sing goodbye to X* [puppet's name].'

Goodbye X, goodbye X,

Goodbye everyone,

We'll see you all next time.

A Musical Day Out – further ideas

'ONE CHILD WENT TO MOW' SONG AND ACTIVITY

Lesson objectives **Listening for your name, then stepping into the circle if you hear it.**

One child stands in the middle of the circle pretending to mow a field, and is joined, one by one, by up to four others – at the most, to keep the song from getting too complex – as their name is called.

One child went to mow,
Went to mow a meadow,
One child and his/her friend [*Sally*, for example]
Went to mow a meadow.

Two children went to mow,
Went to mow a meadow,
Two children, one child and his/her friend [*Peter*, for example], etc.

'DRIVE, DRIVE, DRIVE'

See 'The Park' theme (pages 56–57).

'FIVE LITTLE DUCKS GO SWIMMING ALONG'

See 'The Park' theme (page 58).

'MATCH THE MUSIC'

See 'A Day at Home' theme (page 34).

3. The Park (Version 1)

Resources

Into the Listening Box, put:

- toy ducks
- large piece of blue material for a pond
- toy frog.

You will also need:

- shakers, e.g. bells and rattles.

Starter activity

Introduce your puppet, why you are all here and what you mean by 'good listening'. For example: *'Hello, this is X* [puppet's name]. *Can you see his/her big ears? That's so he/she can be a "good listener". We're all going to do some "good listening" with X today. "Good listening" is:*

- ☐ *not talking*
- ☐ *sitting still*
- ☐ *looking at who is talking*
- ☐ *thinking about the words.*

Well done, Y [child's name], *you are sitting still – that's "good listening"!'*

Throughout the group session you should look out for children exhibiting 'good listening' skills and praise them in this way as a positive method of reminding the whole group what is expected of them. It is harder to tell if a child is 'thinking about the words', but praise them for this if, for example, they put their duck on the pond at the right time during the 'Five little ducks' song and activity on page 58.

HELLO SONG

Lesson objectives — **To signal the beginning of the group session, gaining the children's attention and interest for taking part in the following activities.**

Main activity

Say: *'Let's all sing "hello" to X* [puppet's name]*, and make him/her feel welcome.'*

> Hello X, hello X,
>
> Hello everyone,
>
> It's nice to see you here.

- Prompt for 'good listening'. Praise anyone who, for example, is *'...looking at me – well done, that's "good listening".'*

'WHAT'S IN THE LISTENING BOX TODAY?' SONG AND ACTIVITY

Lesson objectives **Listening and/or looking at clues to the contents of the box. Also introduces the theme for the session.**

Main activity

Encourage the children to clap as you sing the song to get their attention, and get them involved even before they have learned the words. Say: 'X [puppet's name] *has brought along his/her Listening Box. I wonder what's in it today? Let's clap along to the song!'*

What's in the Listening Box today?

What's in the Listening Box today?

What's in the Listening Box today?

What's in the Listening Box?

After the song, keep the children's attention by making a big thing about what you've got hidden in the Listening Box. Tell the children that you are going to make the noise of something in the box and they have to guess what it is. Make the noise of a duck and say: *'What do you think it is?'* If a child guesses correctly, bring the duck out of the box and make its noise again to help the children match it to the toy duck, particularly for those who may be unable to do this. If none of the children guesses the animal correctly, make the noise again. If they still have not guessed after hearing it twice, make the noise again, and at the same time bring the animal briefly out of the box to give the children a visual prompt. If they still are unable to guess, show them a duck, name it and make its noise to help the child to learn.

- Repeat the activity about six times (making the frog noise, and bringing out the frog once or twice as a contrasting sound, or the activity will be too easy); no more than this or you may lose the children's attention.

✓

- To avoid distracting the children from the main activity, wait until you have finished the activity before giving out a duck to each child and keeping one for yourself, for demonstration purposes. So that they attend and listen to the introduction to the next activity, tell them to leave their ducks on the floor in front of them until you say that they can pick them up.
- Make sure the children have understood what the theme for the session is by summarizing as follows: *'So where do you think X* [puppet's name] *is taking us today? Somewhere you might see ducks.* [Pause to give the children a chance to guess.] *We're going to the park!'* [Or pond or canal, if one of these is suggested by a child.]
- Prompt for 'good listening'. Praise anyone who, for example, is *'...not talking – well done, that's good listening.'*

'DRIVE, DRIVE, DRIVE' SONG AND ACTIVITY

Lesson objectives **Looking and listening for a change of speed in a song, and responding accordingly.**

Main activity

Say: *'Let's go to the park in the car. Everyone get in your car and hold on to the steering wheel. Sometimes the car will go slowly* [demonstrate steering the car slowly] *and sometimes it will go fast* [demonstrate] *– watch and listen to find out.'*

Drive, drive, drive,

Drive, drive, drive,

Beep beep, toot toot,

Drive, drive, drive'.

(Sing this verse three times, and use a different speed each time, i.e. slow, medium or fast.)

- Link to the next activity. Say: *'Whew, we made it to the park, although we were going a bit fast!'*
- Prompt for 'good listening'. Praise anyone who, for example, is *'...sitting still – well done, that's "good listening".'*

'HAVE YOU SEEN THE LITTLE DUCKS?' SONG AND ACTIVITY

Lesson objectives Matching actions to words in the song.

- Spread the 'pond' out on the floor in the middle of the circle and put a few ducks on it.

Main activity

Say: *'Look over there, there are ducks on the pond. Have you ever been to feed the ducks? – Have you noticed what they like to do?'* Demonstrate the different actions that the ducks do in the song (i.e. swimming, dipping their beaks in the water, flapping their wings) either by miming or by making the toy ducks do it. Encourage the children to have a go at the actions too. Then say: *'Now we are going to learn a rhyme about the ducks and what they like to do; let's do the actions at the same time!'*

(recite as a poem)

Have you seen the little ducks?
Swimming on the water,
Mother, father, baby ducks,
Swimming on the water.

Have you seen them *dip their beaks*?
Swimming on the water,
Mother, father, baby ducks,
Swimming on the water.

Have you seen them *flap their wings*?
Swimming on the water,
Mother, father, baby ducks,
Swimming on the water.

- Prompt for 'good listening'.

'FIVE LITTLE DUCKS GO SWIMMING ALONG' SONG AND ACTIVITY

Lesson objectives **Listening for children's own names in the song, and each demonstrating that they have heard their name by carrying out a specific action, i.e. putting a duck on the 'pond'.**

Main activity

Say: *'Now we're going to sing about "Five little ducks"; you need to listen out for your name in the song and, if you hear it, put your duck on the pond* [demonstrate].'

If you have another adult running the group with you, call out their name during the first verse, so that they can demonstrate what to do for the children.

(to the tune of 'Bobby Shaftoe')

Five little ducks go swimming along
Swim swim swim, go swimming along
One little duck belongs to [child's name]
Here comes [child's name]'s duck.

Four little ducks go swimming along, etc.
...Here comes [child's name]'s duck.

Three little ducks...etc.
Here comes [child's name]'s duck.

Two little ducks...etc.
Here comes [child's name]'s duck.

One little duck...etc.
Here comes [child's name]'s duck.

All the little ducks go swimming along
Swim swim swim, go swimming along
All the little ducks go swimming along
Here come all the ducks! [The rest of the children get to put their ducks on the 'pond'.]

- Prompt for 'good listening'.

'LITTLE RIPPLES' SONG AND ACTIVITY

(with thanks to Sue Smith for permission to use her adapted version of the 'Little ripples' rhyme.)

Lesson objectives **Children listen for the concepts 'big'/'little' and 'noisy'/'quiet' and join in accordingly.**

Main activity

Say: *'It's getting windy now, the ducks are going in* [collect ducks in but leave the pond out]. *The wind is making quiet little ripples* [demonstrate by rippling the "pond" material] *and big noisy waves* [demonstrate] *on the pond. Listen to the words of the song, hold on to the edge of the pond and make the quiet little ripples and big noisy waves as we sing about them.'*

> Little ripples, little ripples, rippling up and down (sing quietly),
> Little ripples, little ripples, rippling all around.
>
> Big waves, big waves, splashing up and down (sing loudly),
> Big waves, big waves, splashing all around.

- Put the 'pond' away and give out the instruments. Tell the children to leave them on the floor until you say to pick them up. Make sure that you and your colleagues have an instrument each too, but leave yours on the floor as a good model for the children.
- Prompt for 'good listening'.

'SHAKE 'N' SHAKE' SONG AND ACTIVITY

Lesson objectives **Listening for and responding to the word 'Stop'.**

Main activity

Say: *'After all that wind, we are very cold, and a bit wet from all the splashing! – Let's sing a shaky song to warm us up!'* Tell the children to listen out for the word 'Stop' in the song. Say: *'When you hear the word "Stop"* [put your hand up in a "stop" gesture as an extra, visual prompt], *stop shaking your instrument.'*

(to the tune of 'Here we go round the mulberry bush')

Shake and shake and shake and shake,

Shake and shake, shake and shake,

Shake and shake and shake and STOP [*visual prompt*].

Shake and shake and shake.
Let's go up, let's go down, in the air, on the ground,

Shake it, shake it all around.

In your lap, shhh [*index finger to lips as a visual prompt*], don't make a sound.

- Collect all the instruments and put them away to reduce any distraction.
- Prompt for 'good listening'.

SONG: 'TWINKLE, TWINKLE, LITTLE STAR'

Lesson objectives **Settling the children down at the end of what may have been an exciting session for them.**

Main activity

Say: *'It's late now, time for the stars to come out and for us to rest. Here are my stars* [demonstrate the action for the song, i.e. holding up fingers and making a twinkling movement with them], *can you show me yours?'*

Twinkle, twinkle, little star,

How I wonder what you are,

Up above the world so high,

Like a diamond in the sky.

Twinkle, twinkle, little star,

How I wonder what you are.

GOODBYE SONG

Lesson objectives **To signal the end of the group session.**

Main activity

Say: *'And now it's the end of the day and X* [puppet's name] *has to go home, so let's sing goodbye to him/her.'*

Goodbye X, goodbye X,

Goodbye everyone,

We'll see you all next time.

The Park (Version 2)

Resources

Into the Listening Box, put:

- toy ducks
- large piece of blue material for a pond
- toy frog.

You will also need:

- shakers, e.g. bells and rattles.

Starter activity

Say: *'Hello, this is X* [puppet's name]. *Can you see his/her big ears? That's so he/she can be a "good listener". We're all going to do some "good listening" with X today. "Good listening" is:*

- ☐ *not talking*
- ☐ *sitting still*
- ☐ *looking at who is talking*
- ☐ *thinking about the words.*

Well done, Y [child's name], *you are sitting still – that's "good listening"!'*

HELLO SONG

Main activity

Say: *'Let's all sing "hello" to X* [puppet's name], *and make him/her feel welcome.'*

> Hello X, hello X,
>
> Hello everyone,
>
> It's nice to see you here.

- Prompt for 'good listening'.

'WHAT'S IN THE LISTENING BOX TODAY?' SONG AND ACTIVITY

Main activity

Say: 'X [puppet's name] *has brought along his/her Listening Box. I wonder what's in it today? Let's clap along to the song,'* and model this for the children as you sing.

> What's in the Listening Box today?
>
> What's in the Listening Box today?
>
> What's in the Listening Box today?
>
> What's in the Listening Box?

- Say: *'I am going to make the noise of something in this box – try to guess what it is.'*
- Make the noise of a duck (or frog once or twice) and allow the children to guess, saying: *'What do you think it is?'* Repeat.
- Give out a duck to each child but keep one for yourself, for demonstration purposes. Say: *'Leave the ducks on the floor until I tell you to pick them up.'*
- Say: *'So where do you think X* [puppet's name] *is taking us today? Somewhere you might see ducks. We're going to the park!* [or pond, or canal].'
- Prompt for 'good listening'.

'DRIVE, DRIVE, DRIVE' SONG AND ACTIVITY

Main activity

Say: *'Let's go to the park in the car. Everyone get in your car and hold on to the steering wheel. Sometimes the car will go slowly* [demonstrate] *and sometimes it will go fast* [demonstrate]. *Watch and listen to find out.'*

> Drive, drive, drive,
> Drive, drive drive,
> Beep, beep, toot toot,
> Drive, drive, drive.
>
> (Sing this verse three times, and use a different speed each time, i.e. slow, medium or fast.)

- Link to the next activity. Say: *'Whew, we made it to the park, although we were going a bit fast!'*
- Prompt for 'good listening'.

'HAVE YOU SEEN THE LITTLE DUCKS?' SONG AND ACTIVITY

Main activity

Spread the 'pond' out on the floor and put a few ducks on it.
Say: *'Look over there, there are ducks on the pond. Have you ever been to feed the ducks? Have you noticed what they like to do? They like to swim* [demonstrate], *and dip their beaks in the water* [demonstrate], *and flap their wings* [demonstrate]. *Have a go yourselves. Now we are going to learn a rhyme about the ducks and what they like to do; let's do the actions at the same time!'*

> (recite as poem)
>
> Have you seen the little ducks?
> *Swimming* on the water,
> Mother, father, baby ducks,
> Swimming on the water.

Have you seen them *dip their beaks*?
Swimming on the water,
Mother, father, baby ducks,
Swimming on the water.

Have you seen them *flap their wings*?
Swimming on the water,
Mother, father, baby ducks,
Swimming on the water.

- Prompt for 'good listening'.

'FIVE LITTLE DUCKS GO SWIMMING ALONG' SONG AND ACTIVITY

Main activity

Say: *'Now we're going to sing about five little ducks; you need to listen out for your name in the song, and if you hear it, put your duck on the pond* [demonstrate].*'*

(to the tune of 'Bobby Shaftoe')

Five little ducks go swimming along
Swim swim swim, go swimming along
One little duck belongs to [child's name]
Here comes [child's name]'s duck.

Four little ducks go swimming along, etc.
...Here comes [child's name]'s duck.

Three little ducks...etc.
Here comes [child's name]'s duck.

Two little ducks...etc.
Here comes [child's name]'s duck.

✓

One little duck…etc.
Here comes [child's name]'s duck.
All the little ducks go swimming along
Swim swim swim, go swimming along
All the little ducks go swimming along
Here come all the ducks! [The rest of the children get to put their ducks on the 'pond'.]

- Prompt for 'good listening'.

'LITTLE RIPPLES' SONG AND ACTIVITY

Main activity

Say: *'It's getting windy now, the ducks are going in* [collect ducks in] *and there are quiet little ripples* [demonstrate] *and big noisy waves* [demonstrate] *on the pond. Listen to the words of the song, hold on to the edge of the pond and make the little ripples and big waves as we sing about them.'*

Little ripples, little ripples, rippling up and down (sing quietly),
Little ripples, little ripples, rippling all around.

Big waves, big waves, splashing up and down (sing loudly),
Big waves, big waves, splashing all around.

- Put the 'pond' away and give out the instruments – say: *'Leave your instrument on the floor until I say to pick it up.'*
- Prompt for 'good listening'.

'SHAKE 'N' SHAKE' SONG AND ACTIVITY

Main activity

Say: 'After all that wind, we are very cold, and a bit wet from all the splashing! – Let's sing a shaky song to warm us up!'

Also say: *'When you hear the word "Stop"* [put your hand up in a "stop" gesture as an extra, visual prompt], *stop shaking your instrument.'*

(to the tune of 'Here we go round the mulberry bush')

Shake and shake and shake and shake,

Shake and shake, shake and shake,

Shake and shake and shake and STOP [*visual prompt*].

Shake and shake and shake.

Let's go up, let's go down, in the air, on the ground,

Shake it, shake it all around.

In your lap, shhh [*visual prompt*], don't make a sound.

- Put the instruments away.
- Prompt for 'good listening'.

SONG: 'TWINKLE, TWINKLE, LITTLE STAR'

Main activity

Say: *'It's late now, time for the stars to come out and for us to rest. Here are my stars* [demonstrate]; *can you show me yours?* [prompt]'.

Twinkle, twinkle, little star,

How I wonder what you are,

Up above the world so high,

Like a diamond in the sky.
Twinkle, twinkle, little star,

How I wonder what you are.

GOODBYE SONG

Main activity

Say: *'And now it's the end of the day and X* [puppet's name] *has to go home, so let's sing goodbye to him/her.'*

Goodbye X, goodbye X,

Goodbye everyone,

We'll see you all next time.

The Park – further ideas

NAME AND ROLL ACTIVITY

Children take turns to roll a ball to each other, but before rolling they call another child's name, so that they are ready to catch it (if they're listening!).

'THIS LITTLE TRAIN' SONG AND ACTIVITY

See 'A Musical Day Out' theme (page 39).

'KITES FLY WAY UP HIGH' SONG AND ACTIVITY

See 'A Musical Day Out' theme (page 40).

'LET'S ALL HAVE A PICNIC' SONG AND ACTIVITY

See 'A Musical Day Out' theme (page 40).

'ONE CHILD WENT TO MOW' SONG AND ACTIVITY

See 'A Musical Day Out' theme (page 52).

✓

4. The Farm (Version 1)

RESOURCES

Into the Listening Box, put:

- toy pigs
- toy sheep
- toy cows
- toy horses.

You will also need:

- shakers.

Starter activity

Introduce your puppet, why you are all here and what you mean by 'good listening'. For example: *'Hello, this is X* [puppet's name]. *Can you see his/her big ears? That's so he/she can be a "good listener". We're all going to do some "good listening" with X today. "Good listening" is:*

- ☐ *not talking*
- ☐ *sitting still*
- ☐ *looking at who is talking*
- ☐ *thinking about the words.*

Well done, Y [child's name], *you are sitting still – that's "good listening"!'*

Throughout the group session you should look out for children exhibiting 'good listening' skills and praise them in this way as a positive method of reminding the whole group what is expected of them. It is harder to tell if a child is 'thinking about the words' but praise them for this if they, for example, lift up their animal when you say its name in the introduction to 'Old MacDonald' on pages 72–73.

HELLO SONG

Lesson objectives **To signal the beginning of the group session, gaining the children's attention and interest for taking part in the following activities.**

Main activity

Say: *'Let's all sing "hello" to X* [puppet's name], *and make him/her feel welcome.'*

Hello X, hello X,

Hello everyone,

It's nice to see you here.

- Prompt for 'good listening'. Tell the children to 'listen'. Praise anyone who, for example, is *'...not talking – well done, that's "good listening".'*

'WHAT'S IN THE LISTENING BOX TODAY?' SONG AND ACTIVITY

Lesson objectives **Listening and/or looking at clues to the contents of the box. Also introduces the theme for the session.**

Main activity

Encourage the children to clap as you sing the song to get their attention and get them involved even before they have learned the words. Say: *'X* [puppet's name] *has brought along his/her Listening Box. I wonder what's in it today? Let's clap along as we sing the song.'*

What's in the Listening Box today?

What's in the Listening Box today?

What's in the Listening Box today?

What's in the Listening Box?

After the song, keep the children's attention by making a big thing about what you've got hidden in the Listening Box. Tell them that you are going to make the noise of something in the box and they have to guess what it is. Make the noise of one of the animals and say: *'What do you think it is?'*

If a child guesses correctly, bring the animal out of the box and make its noise again to match it to the animal, particularly for those who are unable to do this. If none of the children guesses the animal correctly, make the noise again. If they still have not guessed after hearing it twice, make the noise again and at the same time bring the animal briefly out of the box to give the children a visual prompt. If they still are unable to guess the name of the animal, show them, say its name and make its noise to help the children to learn it.

- Repeat the activity for four to six different (or some repeated) animals in the Listening Box. No more than this or you may lose the children's attention.
- To avoid distracting the children from the main activity, wait until you have finished the activity before giving out an animal to each child; keep a set for yourself, for demonstration purposes. So that they attend and listen to the introduction to the next activity, tell them to leave their animals on the floor in front of them until you say that they can pick them up.
- Make sure the children have understood what the theme for the session is by summarizing as follows: *'So where do you think X* [puppet's name] *is taking us today, somewhere you can see all these animals?* [Pause to give the children a chance to guess.] *Today X is taking us to the farm.'*
- Prompt for 'good listening'.

'OLD MACDONALD' SONG AND ACTIVITY

Lesson objectives **Listening for the animals' names and matching them to the animals in the children's hands.**

Main activity

Tell the children that they can pick up their animals, that you are all going to sing 'Old MacDonald had a farm', and that if you say the name of their animal, they must hold it up for everyone to see. Make sure that all the children know which animal they have and that they have understood

what they have to do by saying: *'So if I sing "and on his farm he had a cow", who's got a cow? Hold it up for everyone to see!'* – and similarly go through all the other animals the children have. It is good practice, if you have enough of each animal, to have one of each type yourself to hold up, to give the children an extra, visual prompt as to which animal is being named, whether it is the same animal as the one they have, and what to do if it is.

Old MacDonald had a farm,

E–I–E–I–O.

And on that farm he had a cow [*prompt the children who have cows to hold them up*],

E–I–E–I–O.

With a moo, moo, here

And a moo, moo, there

Here a moo, there a moo,

Everywhere a moo, moo.

Old MacDonald had a farm,

E–I–E–I–O.

[etc. for each animal type]

- Tell the children to put their animals down on the floor in front of them.
- Prompt for 'good listening'. Tell the children to 'listen'. Praise anyone who, for example, is '*...sitting still – well done, that's "good listening".*'

'BOUNCE, BOUNCE, BOUNCE' SONG AND ACTIVITY

Lesson objectives **Listening for fast vs. slow rates of singing, and joining in accordingly.**

Main activity

Tell the children to get into their tractors [*mime holding the steering wheel for them to copy*], because they are all going to drive across the fields to where the animals are. Tell them that the fields have lots of stones and when they drive over them it will make them bounce and wriggle in their seats [*mime a bouncing and then wriggling action as you hold your wheel*]. Tell them also that sometimes they will be going uphill, so the tractor will go very slowly [*mime slowly turning the steering wheel and bouncing/wriggling*] and sometimes they will be going downhill, so the tractor will go fast [*mime turning the steering wheel quickly and bouncing/wriggling*].

Say: *'So let's take a tractor ride to the field and sing a bouncy song. Remember to bounce and wriggle in your tractor! Slowly first – we're going up the hill.'*

Bounce, bounce, bounce,

Bounce, bounce, bounce,

Wriggle, wriggle, wriggle, wriggle,

Bounce, bounce, bounce.

Say: *'Now faster – we're going down a hill.'*

Bounce, bounce, bounce,

Bounce, bounce, bounce,

Wriggle, wriggle, wriggle, wriggle,

Bounce, bounce, bounce.

Say: *'Now slowly again, because we're nearly there.'*

> Bounce, bounce, bounce,
>
> Bounce, bounce, bounce,
>
> Wriggle, wriggle, wriggle, wriggle,
>
> Bounce, bounce, bounce.

Say: *'We've got to the field where the animals live, let's give them some food.'* Pretend to feed your animal out of your hand, and give the children a chance to do the same to their animals.

- Prompt for 'good listening'. Tell the children to 'listen'. Praise anyone who, for example, is *'...looking at me – well done, that's "good listening".'*

GUESS THE ANIMAL ACTIVITY

Lesson objectives **Listening to other children and matching a noise to an animal.**

Main activity

Tell the children to have a good look at what animal they have, talk to them about each one and remind them what noise they make. Then tell the children to hide their animals behind their backs. Say: *'Oh dear, I think it's going to rain, so all the animals are hiding in the trees – I wonder if they will come out if we guess where they are! I am going to make my animal's noise – if you can guess what animal I have got it will come out!'*

Make your animal's noise, giving the children a visual clue (e.g. a quick peek at the animal) if they need some help, and when someone has guessed correctly, bring the animal out and make the noise, with the animal in sight, to support the learning of those who were unable to guess. If you feel the children need a further demonstration of how the game is played, get a colleague who is helping to run your group to take the next turn. Let about five children each have a turn. Just before each child has a turn, remind the others to listen to the one making the noise, i.e. say: *'Everyone else listen to Y* [child's name].*'*

At the end of the activity, tell the children that it has started to rain on the farm now, so the animals want to go indoors. Get the children to stay sitting where they are and go round the circle to collect all the animals back into the Listening Box. Give out the shakers, encouraging the children to put them on the floor in front of them, to reduce distraction. Make sure that you and your colleagues have a shaker each too, but leave yours on the floor as a good model for the children.

'I HEAR THUNDER' SONG AND ACTIVITY

Lesson objectives **Listening to the difference between 'noisy' and 'quiet' sounds and joining in accordingly.**

Main activity

Tell them how rain can be a quiet sound, and make a quiet sound with your shaker. Then tell them how thunder makes a noisy sound, and make a loud sound with your shaker. Then tell the children to pick up their shakers and join in as you make a quiet 'rain' sound and a noisy 'thunder' sound. Tell them that you are all going to sing a song in which there will be rain and thunder, and they are to make quiet and noisy sounds with their shakers along with the song.

(to the tune of 'Frère Jacques')

I hear thunder [*loud sound*],

I hear thunder [*loud sound*].

Hark, don't you? [*loud sound*]

Hark, don't you? [*loud sound*]

Pitter, patter, raindrops [*quiet sound – put your index finger to your lips as a visual prompt for 'quiet'*],

Pitter, patter, raindrops [*quiet sound*].

I'm wet through [*quiet sound*],

So are you [*quiet sound*].

After the song, tell the children to put the instruments back down on the floor until you say to pick them up.

- Prompt for 'good listening'.

'SHAKE 'N' SHAKE' SONG AND ACTIVITY

Lesson objectives   Listening for and responding to the word 'Stop'.

Main activity

Say: *'After all that rain we're wet and cold – let's sing a shaky song to warm us up!'* Tell the children to listen out for the word 'Stop' in the song. Say: *'When you hear the word "Stop"* [put your hand up in a "stop" gesture as an extra, visual prompt] *stop shaking your shaker.'*

(to the tune of'Here we go round the mulberry bush')

Shake and shake and shake and shake,

Shake and shake, shake and shake,

Shake and shake and shake and STOP [*visual prompt*].

Shake and shake and shake.

Let's go up, let's go down, in the air, on the ground,

Shake it, shake it all around.

In your lap, shhh [*index finger to lips as a visual prompt*], don't make a sound.

- Collect all the shakers and put them away.
- Prompt for 'good listening'.

SONG: 'TWINKLE, TWINKLE, LITTLE STAR'

Lesson objectives **To settle the children at the end of the session – especially important if they have become excited.**

Main activity

Say: *'It's getting late and the stars are coming out – here are my stars* [put your fingers up and twinkle them like stars], *have you got yours?* [Prompt the children to put their fingers up too.] *Let's sing about our stars!'*

Twinkle, twinkle, little star,

How I wonder what you are,

Up above the world so high,

Like a diamond in the sky.

Twinkle, twinkle, little star,

How I wonder what you are.

GOODBYE SONG

Lesson objectives **To signal the end of the group session.**

Main activity

Say: *'And now let's sing goodbye to X* [puppet's name].*'*

Goodbye X, goodbye X,

Goodbye everyone,

We'll see you all next time.

The Farm (Version 2)

Resources

Into the Listening Box, put:

- toy pigs
- toy sheep
- toy cows
- toy horses.

You will also need:

- shakers.

Starter activity

Say: *'Hello, this is X* [puppet's name]. *Can you see his/her big ears? That's so he/she can be a "good listener". We're all going to do some "good listening" with X today. "Good listening" is:*

☐ *not talking*

☐ *sitting still*

☐ *looking at who is talking*

☐ *thinking about the words.*

Well done, Y [child's name], *you are sitting still – that's "good listening"!'*

HELLO SONG

Main activity

Say: *'Let's all sing hello to X* [puppet's name], *and make him/her feel welcome.'*

Hello X, hello X,

Hello everyone,

It's nice to see you here.

- Prompt for 'good listening'.

'WHAT'S IN THE LISTENING BOX TODAY?' SONG AND ACTIVITY

Main activity

Say: 'X [puppet's name] *has brought along his/her Listening Box. I wonder what's in it today. Let's clap along as we sing the song.'*

What's in the Listening Box today?

What's in the Listening Box today?

What's in the Listening Box today?

What's in the Listening Box?

- Say: *'I am going to make the noise of something in this box – try to guess what it is.'*
- Make the noise of a farm animal and allow the children to guess. Say: *'What do you think it is?'* Repeat about five times, once or twice per animal type.
- Give each child a farm animal but keep a set for yourself, for demonstration purposes. Say: *'Leave them on the floor until I say.'* Then say: *'So where do you think X* [puppet's name] is taking us today, somewhere where you can see all these animals? [Pause.] *Today X is taking us to the farm!'*

✓

'OLD MACDONALD' SONG AND ACTIVITY

Main activity

Say: *'Pick up your animals. Let's sing "Old MacDonald had a farm"; when you hear us sing the name of your animal, hold it up like this* [demonstrate], *for everyone to see.'*

Make sure that all the children know which animal they have, then say: *'So if you hear us sing about a cow, hold your cow up in the air, like this* [demonstrating for each animal type in turn].'

> Old MacDonald had a farm,
>
> E–I–E–I–O.
>
> And on that farm he had a cow [*prompt the children who have cows to hold them up*],
>
> E–I–E–I–O.
>
> With a moo, moo, here
>
> And a moo, moo, there
>
> Here a moo, there a moo
>
> Everywhere a moo, moo.
>
> Old MacDonald had a farm,
>
> E–I–E–I–O.
>
> [etc. for each animal type]

- Say: *'Put your animals down on the floor in front of you.'*
- Prompt for 'good listening'.

'BOUNCE, BOUNCE, BOUNCE' SONG AND ACTIVITY

Main activity

Say: *'The animals need feeding now, so let's take a bumpy ride across the fields in our tractors to give them some food. Get into your tractor* [demonstrate]. *As we drive over the stones in the field, we are going to bounce up and down and wriggle in our seats – sometimes we'll go up a hill slowly* [demonstrate] *and sometimes we'll go down a hill very fast* [demonstrate]*; listen and watch as we sing the song.'* Then say: *'So let's take a tractor ride to the field and sing a bouncy song. Remember to bounce and wriggle in your tractor! Slowly first – we're going up the hill.'*

Bounce, bounce, bounce,

Bounce, bounce, bounce,

Wriggle, wriggle, wriggle, wriggle,

Bounce, bounce, bounce.

Say: *'Now faster – we're going down a hill.'*

Bounce, bounce, bounce,

Bounce, bounce, bounce,

Wriggle, wriggle, wriggle, wriggle,

Bounce, bounce, bounce.

Say: *'Now slowly again, because we're nearly there.'*

Bounce, bounce, bounce,

Bounce, bounce, bounce,

Wriggle, wriggle, wriggle, wriggle,

Bounce, bounce, bounce.

Say: 'We've got to the field where the animals live, let's give them some food' [demonstrate].

- Prompt for 'good listening'.

GUESS THE ANIMAL ACTIVITY

Main activity

Say: *'Have a look at what animal you have – what noise does it make? Now hide your animals behind your backs. Oh dear, I think it's going to rain, so all the animals are hiding in the trees – I wonder if they will come out if we guess where they are! I am going to make my animal's noise – if you can guess what animal I've got, it will come out!'* [demonstrate].

Then about five of the children have a turn; say each time: *'Everyone else listen to Y* [child's name]*.'* After the activity, say: *'It has started to rain on the farm now, so the animals want to go indoors. Stay sitting where you are, and I will come and collect them.'*

- Give out the shakers and say: *'Leave your shakers on the floor until I say to pick them up.'*

'I HEAR THUNDER' SONG AND ACTIVITY

Main activity

Say: *'Oh dear, it is raining* and *thundering on the farm now. Listen while I make a quiet sound like rain* [demonstrate] *and a noisy sound like thunder* [demonstrate].*'*

Then say: *'Pick up your shakers and join in with a quiet rain sound* [demonstrate], *and then a noisy thunder sound* [demonstrate].*'*

Then say: *'Now let's sing a song; listen and watch for the quiet and noisy sounds and join in with your instruments.'*

(to the tune of Frère Jacques')

I hear thunder [*loud sound*],

I hear thunder [*loud sound*].

Hark, don't you? [*loud sound*]

Hark, don't you? [*loud sound*]

Pitter, patter, raindrops [*quiet sound and visual prompt*],

Pitter, patter, raindrops [*quiet sound*].

I'm wet through [*quiet sound*],

So are you [*quiet sound*].

Say: *'Put your instruments down on the floor in front of you again until I say to pick them up.'*

- Prompt for 'good listening'.

'SHAKE 'N' SHAKE' SONG AND ACTIVITY

Main activity

Say: *'After all that rain we're wet and cold – let's sing a shaky song to warm us up! When you hear the word "Stop"* [visual prompt], *stop shaking your shaker.'*

(to the tune of 'Here we go round the mulberry bush')

Shake and shake and shake and shake,

Shake and shake, shake and shake,

Shake and shake and shake and STOP.

- Put away the shakers.
- Prompt for 'good listening'.

SONG: 'TWINKLE, TWINKLE, LITTLE STAR'

Main activity

Say: *'It's getting late and the stars are coming out – here are my stars* [demonstrate], *have you got yours? Let's sing about our stars!'*

Twinkle, twinkle, little star,

How I wonder what you are,

Up above the world so high,

Like a diamond in the sky.

Twinkle, twinkle, little star,

How I wonder what you are.

GOODBYE SONG

Main activity

Say: *'And now let's sing goodbye to X* [puppet's name].*'*

Goodbye X, goodbye X,

Goodbye everyone,

We'll see you all next time.

The Farm – further ideas

OBJECT/SOUND MATCHING ACTIVITY

Each child has an animal toy (or animal peg puzzle piece or animal fuzzy-felt piece). The group leader makes an animal sound and the children have to work out whether it's their animal's sound. If so, the children put their toys in a 'field' (piece of green material), or insert their puzzle piece into its puzzle, or stick their fuzzy-felt piece onto its board.

TOSS THE ANIMAL (BEAN BAGS) ACTIVITY

Each child has an animal, preferably a beanie animal. A hoop or a large basket or box, or a sheet of green material, is placed in the middle of the circle as a 'field' or 'shed'. The children listen for:

a. their animal's name, or

b. their animal's noise, or

c. ready, steady, go!

before throwing their animals into the 'field' or 'shed'.

'FIVE LITTLE DUCKS GO SWIMMING ALONG' SONG AND ACTIVITY

See 'The Park' theme (page 58).

'THIS IS THE WAY WE...' SONG AND ACTIVITY

(to the tune of 'Here we go round the mulberry bush')

This is the way we ride the horse,
Ride the horse, ride the horse.
This is the way we ride the horse,
On a cold and frosty morning.
This is the way we water the plants, etc.
This is the way we drive the tractor, etc.

In this activity, everyone mimes the actions as they sing. Add new words and actions once the children know the original ones well, to keep the children listening and looking – e.g. 'groom the horse' or 'pick the plants'.

5. Birthday (Version 1)

Resources

Into the Listening Box, put:

- shakeable instruments (wrapped).

You will also need:

- beanbags
- basket
- toy food and a plate.

Starter activity

Introduce your puppet, why you are all here and what you mean by 'good listening'. For example: '*Hello, this is X* [puppet's name]. *Can you see his/her big ears? That's so he/she can be a "good listener". We're all going to do some "good listening" with X today. "Good listening" is:*

- ☐ *not talking*
- ☐ *sitting still*
- ☐ *looking at who is talking*
- ☐ *thinking about the words.*

Well done, Y [child's name], *you are sitting still – that's "good listening"!'*

Throughout the group session you should look out for children exhibiting 'good listening' skills and praise them in this way as a positive method of reminding the whole group what is expected of them. It is harder to tell if a child is 'thinking about the words' but praise them for this if they, for example, respond appropriately to the word 'Go' in the beanbag game on pages 94–100.

HELLO SONG

Lesson objectives **To signal the beginning of the group session, gaining the children's attention and interest for taking part in the following activities.**

Main activity

Say: *'Let's all sing hello to X* [puppet's name], *and make him/her feel welcome.'*

Hello X, hello X,

Hello everyone,

It's nice to see you here.

- Prompt for 'good listening'. Tell the children to 'listen'. Praise anyone who, for example, is *'...sitting still – well done, that's "good listening".'*

'WHAT'S IN THE LISTENING BOX TODAY?' SONG AND ACTIVITY

Lesson objectives **Listening and/or looking at clues to the contents of the box. Also introduces the theme for the session.**

Main activity

Encourage the children to clap as you sing the song to get their attention and get them involved even before they have learned the words. Say: *'X* [puppet's name] *has brought along his/her Listening Box. I wonder what's in it today? Let's clap along as we sing the song.'*

What's in the Listening Box today?

What's in the Listening Box today?

What's in the Listening Box today?

What's in the Listening Box?

After the song, keep the children's attention by making a big thing about what you've got hidden in the Listening Box. Say: *'Today there is a special song hidden in the box; I'm going to let it out and I want you to tell me what the song is.'*

Open the Listening Box, then hum the tune of the birthday song. Ask the children to tell you what the song is. If they have difficulty, give the children clues to help them guess. You could hum the tune again or describe something about when they might hear the song – on a day when they are given a special cake with candles on it, for instance. Once they guess, hum the song again, then sing the words to be sure the children have all understood. Then say: *'So today it is X's birthday, so let's sing some songs and play some party games!'*

- Prompt for 'good listening'. Tell the children to 'listen'. Praise anyone who, for example, is *'...looking at me – well done, that's "good listening".'*

'PASS THE PARCEL' SONG AND ACTIVITY

Lesson objectives   Listening for the music to stop before opening a parcel.

Main activity

Say: *'Let's play "Pass the parcel". Pass the parcels around the circle until you hear the music stop, then if you are holding a parcel, open it up and put it on the floor in front of you.'*

Give out a wrapped instrument (or a few all at once if there are more than five children in your group, so that there's more than one parcel going around the circle to keep the children's attention). Also explain to the children that, in this pretend game of 'Pass the parcel', the toys are to be given back afterwards; otherwise, either there will be tears or you will lose some of your resources! Alternatively, you could use shakers made by the children in an earlier creative activity, which the children are allowed to take home.

(to the tune of 'London Bridge is falling down')

Pass the parcel round and round,

Round and round, round and round,

Pass the parcel round and round.

Whose turn is it now?

✓

Say to any child who has opened a parcel: *'Put your shaker on the floor in front of you until I tell you to pick it up.'*

When all the parcels have been opened and all the children have an instrument (making sure that you have one too, for demonstration purposes), say: *'OK, now we have some shakers, pick them up and let's have some birthday fun!'*

- Prompt for 'good listening'. Tell the children to 'listen'. Praise anyone who, for example, is *'...not talking – well done, that's "good listening".'*

'SHAKE 'N' SHAKE' SONG AND ACTIVITY

Lesson objectives   Listening for and responding to the word 'Stop'.

Main activity

Tell the children to listen out for the word 'Stop' in the song. Say: *'Let's sing a shaky song; when you hear the word "Stop" in the song* [put your hand up in a "stop" gesture as an extra, visual prompt], *stop shaking your shaker.'*

(to the tune of 'Here we go round the mulberry bush')

Shake and shake and shake and shake,

Shake and shake, shake and shake,

Shake and shake and shake and STOP [*visual prompt*].

Shake and shake and shake.

Let's go up, let's go down, in the air, on the ground,

Shake it, shake it all around.

In your lap, shhh, don't make a sound [*prompt*].

- Put the shakers away.
- Prompt for 'good listening'.

'LET'S ALL HAVE SOME PARTY FOOD' SONG AND ACTIVITY

Lesson objectives **Listening for the name of the food they are holding and responding accordingly.**

Main activity

Say: *'Time for something to eat at the party.'*

Give out a piece of food to each child (telling them to leave it on the floor) and put the plate in the middle of the circle. Make sure that you keep one of each of the different types of food for demonstration purposes.

Say: *'In the next song, listen out for the name of the food you are holding, and if you hear it, put it on the plate.'* Then say: *'So if we sing "Let's all have some pizza" and you are holding some pizza, who's got some pizza? Put it on the plate like this* [demonstrate].*'* Do this for each type of food that the children have, before you begin the song.

NB: the first verse is just an introduction; no food is placed on the plate until the second verse.

(to the tune of 'Here we go round the mulberry bush')

Let's all have some party food, some party food, some party food,
Let's all have some party food,
Some for you and me.

Let's all have some pizza, some pizza, some pizza,
Let's all have some pizza,
Some pizza for you and me... [etc.]

- Put away the food and plate.
- Prompt for 'good listening'.

THE BEANBAG GAME

Lesson objectives **Listening for the word 'Go' and responding accordingly.**

Main activity

- Give each child a beanbag and put a basket on the floor in the middle of the circle.
- Say: *'Leave the beanbag on the floor until I tell you.'*
- Tell the children that you are all going to play a party game in which they have to listen for you to say *'Ready, steady, go!'* before all trying to throw the beanbag into the basket. Demonstrate by throwing your own beanbag into the basket.
- Say: 'Pick up your beanbags. Now, are you ready? Ready, steady, GO!'
- Say: *'Let's play another party game.'*
- Use visual prompts such as holding up your hand in a STOP position or even placing your hand in the way above the basket, to avoid early throws.
- Repeat for about six throws.

The game can be varied by naming a child before saying *'Ready, steady, go!'* so that the children take turns to throw, but this is harder, as some of them will have to wait and in their excitement may throw too early. You could aim for this level of difficulty once the children are doing well when all throwing together.

- Put away the beanbags and basket.
- Prompt for 'good listening'.

SONG: 'TWINKLE, TWINKLE, LITTLE STAR'

Lesson objectives **To settle the children at the end of the session – especially important if they have become excited.**

Main activity

Say: *'It's getting late and the stars are coming out – here are my stars* [put your hands up and twinkle your fingers like stars], *have you got yours?* [Encourage the children to twinkle their fingers too.] *Let's sing about our stars!'*

> Twinkle, twinkle, little star,
>
> How I wonder what you are,
> Up above the world so high,
>
> Like a diamond in the sky.
>
> Twinkle, twinkle, little star,
>
> How I wonder what you are.

GOODBYE SONG

Lesson objectives **To signal the end of the group session.**

Main activity

Say: *'And now let's sing goodbye to X* [puppet's name].'

> Goodbye X, goodbye X,
>
> Goodbye everyone,
>
> We'll see you all next time.

Birthday (Version 2)

Resources

Into the Listening Box, put:

- shakeable instruments (wrapped).

You will also need:

- beanbags
- basket
- toy food and a plate.

Starter activity

Say: '*Hello, this is X* [puppet's name]. *Can you see his/her big ears? That's so he/she can be a "good listener". We're all going to do some "good listening" with X today. "Good listening" is:*

☐ *not talking*

☐ *sitting still*

☐ *looking at who is talking*

☐ *thinking about the words*

Well done, Y [child's name], *you are sitting still – that's "good listening"!*'

HELLO SONG

Main activity

Say: '*Let's all sing hello to X* [puppet's name], *and make him/her feel welcome.*'

Hello X, hello X,

Hello everyone,

It's nice to see you here.

- Prompt for 'good listening'.

'WHAT'S IN THE LISTENING BOX TODAY?' SONG AND ACTIVITY

Main activity

Say: *'X* [puppet's name] *has brought along his/her Listening Box. I wonder what's in it today. Let's clap along as we sing the song.'*

> What's in the Listening Box today?
>
> What's in the Listening Box today?
>
> What's in the Listening Box today?
>
> What's in the Listening Box?

Then say: *'Today there is a special song hidden in the box; I'm going to let it out and I want you to tell me what the song is.'*

Open the Listening Box, then hum the tune of the birthday song. Say: *'Can anyone tell me what that song is?...* [Pause to give children a chance to guess.]) *'When do we sing it?...When there's a special cake with candles on it...when you get presents...when it's someone's...birthday, yes. It's the birthday song! So today it is X's birthday; let's sing some songs and play some party games!'*

- Prompt for 'good listening'.

'PASS THE PARCEL' SONG AND ACTIVITY

Main activity

Say: *'Let's play* "Pass the parcel"*. Pass the parcels around the circle until you hear the music stop, then if you are holding a parcel, open it up and put it on the floor in front of you.'*

- Give out a wrapped shaker.

✓

(to the tune of 'London Bridge is falling down')

Pass the parcel round and round,

Round and round, round and round,

Pass the parcel round and round.

Whose turn is it now?

Say to any child who has opened a parcel: *'Put your shaker on the floor in front of you until I tell you to pick it up.'* Afterwards say: *'OK, now we have some shakers, pick them up and let's have some birthday fun!'*

- Prompt for 'good listening'.

'SHAKE 'N' SHAKE' SONG AND ACTIVITY

Main activity

Say: *'Let's sing a shaky song; when you hear the word "Stop"* [visual prompt] *in the song, stop shaking your shaker.'*

(to the tune of 'Here we go round the mulberry bush')

Shake and shake and shake and shake,

Shake and shake, shake and shake,

Shake and shake and shake and STOP [*visual prompt*].

Shake and shake and shake.

Let's go up, let's go down, in the air, on the ground,

Shake it, shake it all around.

In your lap, shhh [*visual prompt*], don't make a sound.

- Put the shakers away.
- Prompt for 'good listening'.

'LET'S ALL HAVE SOME PARTY FOOD' SONG AND ACTIVITY

Main activity

Say: *'Time for something to eat at the party.'*

- Give out a piece of food to each child. Say: *'Leave them on the floor until I say to pick them up.'*
- Put the plate in the middle of the circle.
- Say: *'In the next song, listen out for the name of the food you are holding, and if you hear it, put it on the plate.'* Then say: *'So if we sing "Let's all have some pizza..." who's got some pizza? Put it on the plate like this* [demonstrate].*'*

(to the tune of 'Here we go round the mulberry bush)

Let's all have some party food, some party food, some party food,
Let's all have some party food,
Some food for you and me.

Let's all have some pizza, some pizza, some pizza,
Let's all have some pizza,
Some pizza for you and me... [etc.]

- Put away the food and plate.
- Prompt for 'good listening'.

THE BEANBAG GAME

Main activity

Say: *'Let's play another party game.'*

- Give each child a beanbag and put a basket on the floor in the middle of the circle.
- Say: *'Leave the beanbag on the floor until I tell you.'*
- Then say: *'We are all going to play a party game. Listen for me to say "Ready, steady, go!" and when you hear "Go!", throw your beanbag into the basket* [demonstrate]. *Pick up your beanbags. Now, are you ready? Ready...steady...go!'*
- Repeat for about six throws.
- Put away the beanbags and basket.
- Prompt for 'good listening'.

SONG: 'TWINKLE, TWINKLE, LITTLE STAR'

Main activity

Say: *'It's getting late and the stars are coming out – here are my stars* [demonstrate], *have you got yours?* [prompt]. *Let's sing about our stars!'*

Twinkle, twinkle, little star,

How I wonder what you are,

Up above the world so high,

Like a diamond in the sky.

Twinkle, twinkle, little star,

How I wonder what you are.

GOODBYE SONG

Main activity

Say: *'And now let's sing goodbye to X* [puppet's name].*'*

Goodbye X, goodbye X,

Goodbye everyone,

We'll see you all next time.

Birthday – further ideas

MUSICAL STATUES/MUSICAL BUMPS

These traditional games are excellent for encouraging listening and attention skills.

'A NECKLACE FOR X'S BIRTHDAY' SONG AND ACTIVITY

The group leader has some large, easily threaded, colourful beads and some thread, and the children listen for their name before each having a turn threading a bead onto the necklace. This may work better and be more fun with an accompanying song; for example:

(to the tune of 'Here we go round the mulberry bush')

This is how Sara [*for example*] threads the bead,

Threads the bead, threads the bead,

This is how Sara threads the bead,

To make a necklace for X [puppet's name].

POP-UP PIRATE ACTIVITY

Children listen for their name to be called out, to take a turn at putting a sword into the pirate's barrel.

'THIS IS THE WAY WE...' SONG AND ACTIVITY

The children do the actions appropriate to the words. To avoid the children getting too familiar with the song and so reducing the need for them to attend, change the order of the verses sometimes, or put in new verses about things we do at birthday parties.

(to the tune of 'Here we go round the mulberry bush')

This is the way we...blow up balloons,

Blow up balloons, blow up balloons.

This is the way we blow up balloons,

On a cold and frosty morning.

This is the way we...

- ...open the presents
- ...blow out the candles
- ...eat the cake
- ...dance together
- ...play hide and seek

[etc.]

'IF YOU'RE HAPPY AND YOU KNOW IT' (WITH A DIFFERENCE!) SONG AND ACTIVITY

Adapt the song by using actions which differ from the ones which the children are used to, or by putting the actions in a different order. Tell the children beforehand that you are going to do this, and give them a demonstration.

If you're happy and you know it, laugh out loud, ha ha!

If you're happy and you know it, laugh out loud, ha ha!

If you're happy and you know it,

And you really want to show it,
If you're happy and you know it, laugh out loud, ha ha!

If you're happy and you know it, make a big smile…

If you're happy and you know it, clap your hands…

6. The Zoo (Version 1)

Resources:

Into the Listening Box, put zoo animal toys, such as:

- elephant
- lion
- tiger
- seal
- monkey
- spider.

You will also need:

- shakers and bells.

Starter activity

Introduce your puppet, why you are all here and what you mean by 'good listening'. For example: '*Hello, this is X* [puppet's name]. *Can you see his/her big ears? That's so he/she can be a "good listener". We're all going to do some "good listening" with X today. "Good listening" is:*

- ☐ *not talking*
- ☐ *sitting still*
- ☐ *looking at who is talking*
- ☐ *thinking about the words.*

Well done, Y [child's name], *you are sitting still – that's "good listening"!*'

Throughout the group session you should look out for children exhibiting 'good listening' skills and praise them in this way as a positive method of reminding the whole group what is expected of them. It is harder to tell if a child is 'thinking about the words' but praise them for this if they, for example, put their animal in the box at the right time during 'The animals went in two by two' activity on pages 109–110 below.

HELLO SONG

Lesson objectives **To signal the beginning of the group session, gaining the children's attention and interest for taking part in the following activities.**

Main activity

Say: *'Let's all sing hello to X* [puppet's name], *and make him/her feel welcome.'*

> Hello X, hello X,
>
> Hello everyone,
>
> It's nice to see you here.

- Prompt for 'good listening'. Tell the children to 'listen'. Praise anyone who, for example, is *'...sitting still – well done, that's "good listening".'*

'WHAT'S IN THE LISTENING BOX TODAY?' SONG AND ACTIVITY

Lesson objectives **Listening and/or looking at clues to the contents of the box. Also introduces the theme for the session.**

Main activity

Encourage the children to clap as you sing the song to get their attention and get them involved even before they have learned the words.

> What's in the Listening Box today?
>
> What's in the Listening Box today?
>
> What's in the Listening Box today?
>
> What's in the Listening Box?

After the song, keep the children's attention by making a big thing about what you've got hidden in the Listening Box.

Tell them that you are going to make the noise or action (e.g. for the elephant, dangling your arm in front of your face like a trunk) of what is in the box and they have to guess what it is. Make the noise or action of one of the animals and say: *'What do you think it is?'* If a child guesses correctly, bring the animal out of the box and make the noise or action again to match it to the animal, particularly for those who are unable to do this. If none of the children guesses the animal correctly, make the noise or action again. If they still have not guessed after hearing it twice, make the noise or action again, and at the same time bring the animal briefly out of the box to give the children a visual prompt. If they still are unable to guess the name of the animal, show them, say its name and make its noise or action to help the children learn it.

- Repeat the activity with four to six different (or repeated) animals in the Listening Box. No more than this, or you may lose the children's attention.

- To avoid distracting the children from the main activity, wait until you have finished the activity before giving out an animal to each child and keeping a set for yourself, for demonstration purposes. So that they attend and listen to the introduction to the next activity, tell them to leave their animal on the floor in front of them until you say that they can pick them up. Leave yours on the floor also, as a good model for the children.

- Make sure the children have understood what the theme for the session is by summarizing as follows: *'So where do you think X* [puppet's name] *is taking us today, somewhere you can see all these animals?* [Pause to give the children a chance to guess.] *Today X is taking us to the zoo.'*

- Prompt for 'good listening'. Tell the children to 'listen'. Praise anyone who, for example, is *'...looking at me – well done, that's "good listening".'*

'THIS LITTLE TRAIN GOES UP THE HILL' SONG AND ACTIVITY

Lesson objectives Listening for speed of song and responding accordingly.

Main activity

Say: *'How shall we get to the zoo? Let's go by train.'* Tell the children that when the train goes up the hill it goes very slowly, so you will all be singing very slowly; along the top of the hill it will go a bit faster, and then down the hill it will go very fast, it'll be 'racing' along. You can demonstrate the different speeds by doing a train action (i.e. arms by your sides in a right-angle position, then moving forwards in parallel circles like the wheels of the train) at the different speeds as you explain. Say: *'OK, get into your train* [prompt to make train wheels movement with their arms] *and off we go, slowly at first.'*

(to the tune of 'What shall we do with the drunken sailor?') (sing slowly)

This little train goes up the hill,
This little train goes up the hill,
This little train goes up the hill,
This little train goes *slowly*(sing faster).

This little train goes along the top, etc.
This little train goes *faster* (sing very fast).

This little train goes down the hill, etc.
This little train goes *racing*.

- Prompt for 'good listening'. Tell the children to 'listen'. Praise anyone who, for example, is *'...not talking – well done, that's "good listening".'*

GUESS THE ANIMAL ACTIVITY

Lesson objectives **Listening to other children and matching a noise to an animal.**

Main activity

Tell the children to have a good look at what animal they have, talk to them about each one and remind them what noise they make. Then tell them to hide their animals. Then say: *'So here we are at the zoo, but where have all the animals gone? I wonder if they will come out if we guess where they are! I am going to make my animal's noise – see if you can guess what it is!'*

Make your animal's noise, giving the children a visual clue (e.g. a quick peek at the animal) if they need some help, and when someone has guessed correctly, bring the animal out and make the noise with the animal in view to support the learning of those who were unable to guess. If you feel the children need a further demonstration of how the game is played, get a colleague who is helping to run your group to take the next turn. Then let about five children each have a turn. Just before each child has a turn, remind the others to listen to the one making the animal noise, i.e. say: *'Everyone else listen to Y* [child's name].*'*

'THE ANIMALS WENT IN TWO BY TWO' SONG AND ACTIVITY

Lesson objectives **Listening for the name of an animal in the song, and responding accordingly.**

Main activity

Tell the children that it is starting to rain, so the animals want to go indoors. Tell them that they need to listen for the name of the animal they are holding, and when they hear it, put it back in the Listening Box. Demonstrate by saying: *'So if we sing "The elephant and the seal too", who has an elephant and who has a seal?* [hold yours up for the children to see]. *Put them in the box like this.'*

✓

The animals went in two by two,

Hurrah, hurrah,

The animals went in two by two,

Hurrah, hurrah,

The animals went in two by two,

The *elephant* and the *seal* too [*prompt the appropriate children to put their elephants and seals into the box*].

And they all went into the box,

For to get out of the rain.

- Sing the song slowly and stress the animals names so that the children have a better chance of noticing the name of the animal they are holding.
- Repeat the song until all the animals have been named, e.g.

  '...the *monkey* and the *spider* too...'
  '...the *lion* and the *tiger* too...'

- Give out the instruments, again encouraging the children to put them on the floor in front of them rather than holding them and being distracted by them. Make sure that you and your colleagues have an instrument each too, but leave yours on the floor as a good model for the children.

'I HEAR THUNDER' SONG AND ACTIVITY

Lesson objectives **Listening to the difference between 'noisy' and 'quiet' sounds and joining in accordingly.**

Main activity

Tell the children how rain can be a quiet sound, and make a quiet sound with your instrument. Then tell them how thunder makes a noisy sound, and make a loud sound with your instrument. Then tell the children to pick up their instruments and join in as you make a quiet 'rain' sound and a noisy 'thunder' sound. Tell them that you are all going to sing a song in which there will be rain and thunder, and they are to make quiet and noisy sounds with their instruments to match the words in the song.

(to the tune of 'Frère Jacques')

I hear thunder [*loud sound*],

I hear thunder [*loud sound*].

Hark, don't you? [*loud sound*]

Hark, don't you? [*loud sound*]

Pitter, patter, raindrops [*quiet sound – put your index finger to your lips as a visual prompt for 'quiet'*],

Pitter, patter, raindrops [*quiet sound*].

I'm wet through [*quiet sound*],

So are you [*quiet sound*].

- After the song, tell the children to put the instruments back down on the floor until you tell them to pick them up again, to reduce any distraction.
- Prompt for 'good listening'.

'SHAKE 'N' SHAKE' SONG AND ACTIVITY

Lesson objectives **Listening for and responding to the word 'Stop'.**

Main activity

Tell the children to listen out for the word 'Stop' in the song. Say: *'Oh dear, I'm getting cold in this rain, so I'm feeling a bit shivery and shaky. Shall we sing our shaky song to warm us up? When you hear the word "Stop" in the song* [put your hand up in a "stop" gesture as an extra, visual prompt], *stop shaking your instrument.'*

(to the tune of 'Here we go round the mulberry bush')

Shake and shake and shake and shake,

Shake and shake, shake and shake,

Shake and shake and shake and STOP [*visual prompt*].

Shake and shake and shake.

Let's go up, let's go down, in the air, on the ground,

Shake it, shake it all around.

In your lap, shhh [*index finger to lips as a visual prompt*], don't make a sound.

- Put away the instruments.
- Prompt for 'good listening'.

SONG: 'TWINKLE, TWINKLE, LITTLE STAR'

Lesson objectives **To settle the children at the end of the session – especially important if they have become excited.**

Main activity

Say: *'It's getting late and the stars are coming out – here are my stars* [put your fingers up and twinkle them like stars], *have you got yours?* [Encourage the children to put their fingers up too.] *Let's sing about our stars!'*

Twinkle, twinkle, little star,

How I wonder what you are,

Up above the world so high,
Like a diamond in the sky.

Twinkle, twinkle, little star,

How I wonder what you are.

GOODBYE SONG

Lesson objectives **To signal the end of the group session.**

Main activity

Say: *'And now let's sing goodbye to X* [puppet's name].'

Goodbye X, goodbye X,

Goodbye everyone,

We'll see you all next time.

The Zoo (Version 2)

Resources

Into the Listening Box, put zoo animal toys, such as:

- elephant
- lion
- tiger
- seal
- monkey
- spider.

You will also need:

- shakers and bells.

Starter activity

Say: *'Hello, this is X* [puppet's name]. *Can you see his/her big ears? That's so he/she can be a "good listener". We're all going to do some "good listening" with X today. "Good listening" is:*

- ☐ *not talking*
- ☐ *sitting still*
- ☐ *looking at who is talking*
- ☐ *thinking about the words.*

Well done, Y [child's name], *you are sitting still – that's "good listening"!'*

HELLO SONG

Main activity

Say: *'Let's all sing hello to X* [puppet's name], *and make him/her feel welcome.'*

> Hello X, hello X,
>
> Hello everyone,
>
> It's nice to see you here.

- Prompt for 'good listening'.

'WHAT'S IN THE LISTENING BOX TODAY?' SONG AND ACTIVITY

Main activity

Say: 'X [puppet's name] *has brought along his/her Listening Box. I wonder what's in it today? Let's clap along as we sing the song.'*

> What's in the Listening Box today?
>
> What's in the Listening Box today?
>
> What's in the Listening Box today?
>
> What's in the Listening Box?

- Say: *'I am going to make the noise or action of one of the things in the box – try to guess what it is.'*
- Make the noise or action and allow the children time to guess. Say: *'What do you think it is?'*
- Repeat.

- Give out the animals but keep a set for yourself, for demonstration purposes.
- Say: *'Leave them on the floor until I say.'*
- Then say: *'So where do you think X* [puppet's name] *is taking us today, somewhere where you can see all these animals?* [Pause.] *Today X is taking us to the zoo.'*
- Prompt for 'good listening'.

'THIS LITTLE TRAIN GOES UP THE HILL' SONG AND ACTIVITY

Main activity

Say: *'How shall we get to the zoo? Let's go by train.'*

Then say: *'In this next song about the train, first it will go very slowly up a hill, so we must sing very slowly. Then the train goes along the top of the hill, so we sing a bit faster. Then at the end the train goes down the hill, so it goes very fast, it goes racing down the hill* [demonstrate]. *OK, get into your train* [prompt]*, and off we go, slowly at first.'*

(to the tune of 'What shall we do with the drunken sailor?') (sing slowly)

This little train goes up the hill,
This little train goes up the hill,
This little train goes up the hill,
This little train goes *slowly* (sing faster).

This little train goes along the top, etc.
This little train goes *faster* (sing very fast).

This little train goes down the hill, etc.
This little train goes *racing*.

- Prompt for 'good listening'.

GUESS THE ANIMAL ACTIVITY

Main activity

Say: *'Have a look and remember what animal you have – what noise does it make? Now hide your animals behind your backs.'*

Then say: *'So here we are at the zoo, but where have all the animals gone? I wonder if they will come out if we guess where they are! I am going to make my animal's noise – see if you can guess what it is!'*

Give about five children a turn, saying *'Everyone listen to Y* [child's name]*'* each time.

'THE ANIMALS WENT IN TWO BY TWO' SONG AND ACTIVITY

Main activity

Say: *'It has started to rain, so the animals want to go indoors. Listen for the name of the animal you are holding, and when you hear it, put it back in the Listening Box.'*

Demonstrate – say: *'So if we sing "The elephant and the seal too"... who has an elephant and who has a seal? Put them in the box like this.'*

The animals went in two by two,

Hurrah, hurrah,

The animals went in two by two,

Hurrah, hurrah,

The animals went in two by two,

The *elephant* and the *seal* too [*prompt the appropriate children to put their elephants and seals in the box*],

And they all went into the box,

For to get out of the rain.

✓

- Sing the song slowly and stress the animals names so that the children have a better chance of noticing the name of the animal they are holding.
- Give out the instruments. Say: *'Put them on the floor until I tell you to pick them up.'*

'I HEAR THUNDER' SONG AND ACTIVITY

Main activity

Say: *'Listen to the quiet rain noise* [demonstrate], *now listen to the noisy thunder noise* [demonstrate]. *Pick up your instruments and make the different noises with me. Now let's sing a song; listen and watch for the quiet and noisy sounds.'*

(to the tune of 'Frère Jacques')

I hear thunder [*loud sound*],

I hear thunder [*loud sound*].

Hark, don't you? [*loud sound*]

Hark, don't you? [*loud sound*]

Pitter, patter, raindrops [*quiet sound and visual prompt*],

Pitter, patter, raindrops [*quiet sound*].

I'm wet through [*quiet sound*],

So are you [*quiet sound*].

- Prompt for 'good listening'.

'SHAKE 'N' SHAKE' SONG AND ACTIVITY

Main activity

Say: *'Oh dear, I'm getting cold in this rain, so I'm feeling a bit shivery and shaky. Shall we sing our shaky song to warm us up? When you hear the word "Stop" in the song* [prompt], *stop shaking your instrument.'*

(to the tune of 'Here we go round the mulberry bush')

Shake and shake and shake and shake,

Shake and shake, shake and shake,

Shake and shake and shake and STOP [*visual prompt*].

Shake and shake and shake.

Let's go up, let's go down, in the air, on the ground,

Shake it, shake it all around.

In your lap, shhh [*visual prompt*], don't make a sound.

- Prompt for 'good listening'.

SONG: 'TWINKLE, TWINKLE, LITTLE STAR'

Main activity

Say: *'It's getting late and the stars are coming out – here are my stars* [demonstrate], *have you got yours?* [prompt]. *Let's sing about our stars!'*

Twinkle, twinkle, little star,

How I wonder what you are,

Up above the world so high,

Like a diamond in the sky.

Twinkle, twinkle, little star,

How I wonder what you are.

GOODBYE SONG

Main activity

Say: *'And now let's sing goodbye to X* [puppet's name].*'*

Goodbye X, goodbye X,

Goodbye everyone,

We'll see you all next time.

The Zoo – further ideas

'OLD MACDONALD HAD A ZOO' SONG AND ACTIVITY

Activities as for 'The Farm' theme, but using zoo animals, i.e. 'Old MacDonald had a zoo' and putting zoo animal names and their noises into the song.

Old MacDonald had a zoo,

E–I–E–I–O.

And in that zoo he had a *monkey*,

E–I–E–I–O.

With an *ooh ooh* here and an *ooh ooh* there,

Here an *ooh*, there an *ooh*,

Everywhere an *ooh ooh*...

[etc.]

FEED THE ANIMALS ACTIVITY

The children each have a beanbag. Two animals are put in the middle of the circle, some distance apart. Children listen for the name of the animal, or the animal's noise, before throwing it some food (the beanbag). If the children are listening, they will throw the food to the correct animal. (Be aware that any error may be due to throwing skills rather than listening skills, so keeping a good distance between animals reduces confusion.)

'NOISY' AND 'QUIET' ANIMALS ACTIVITY

Explain to the children that some animals are noisy, e.g. elephants, and some are quiet, e.g. butterflies. Use instruments to demonstrate 'noisy' and 'quiet' sounds. Give the children an instrument each. Then use your instrument to be an elephant (noisy) or a butterfly (quiet), and get the

children to guess which animal you are being, from the instrument's sound alone. Then say to the children *'Let's all be elephants'*, or *'Let's all be butterflies'*, and encourage them to join in by making 'noisy' or 'quiet' sounds with their instruments accordingly.

You could vary this by giving the children a turn each and asking: *'Do you want to be an elephant or a butterfly?'* The child chooses, saying their choice out loud (so that you know which one they are aiming for), and makes a 'quiet' or 'noisy' sound with their instrument, depending on what they chose.